POOR RUSSELL'S ALMANAC

Other books by RUSSELL BAKER

....

Washington: City on the Potomac
An American in Washington
No Cause for Panic
All Things Considered
Our Next President
The Upside-down Man
So This Is Depravity

Poor
Russell's
ALMANAC

·······

Russell Baker

CONGDON & LATTÈS
NEW YORK

THE ORIGIN OF
POOR RUSSELL'S
...... ALMANAC ......

Even the most casual reader must soon perceive that a work such as *Poor Russell's Almanac* could not possibly have been the product of a single brain, no matter how enfeebled. It should afford no distress to the public, therefore, to learn that Poor Russell is not a single individual, but the collective pen name for a large group of distinguished men and women who saw the need for a work of this scope and did their utmost to satisfy it.

It would not be entirely correct to describe this distinguished assemblage, as some have already done in the popular press, as "a bunch of eccentrics, and a few old has-beens." There are, to be sure, many eccentrics among them and one or two thoroughly distinguished has-beens, but their range defies the easy cataloguing of which our press is so fond. Suffice it to say, in summing up the *Almanac*'s contributors, creators, authors, poets, prognosticators and philosophers, that they are, each in his own field, persons of great substance whose names are household words wherever connoisseurs of esoterica keep house.

Who, then, someone will ask, are these remarkable ladies and gentlemen who call themselves "Poor Russell"? Most of them, unfortunately, have made it a condition of their employment that their connection with the *Almanac* be kept secret. This is not, despite the usual hastily written assertions of American journalism, because they are ashamed to have their children discover what they have been doing. Far from it. Some, in fact, are perfectly willing to have their involvement exposed, and these we are proud to identify.

The reader will instantly recognize the name of Lady Medea Ainsley, the retired aviatrix who was known throughout England a quarter century ago as "the Epsom Earhart." Aside from contributing much of the *Almanac*'s material dealing with windy spells, quixotic behavior and untimely demise, all subjects that have intensely interested Lady Medea since childhood, she was immensely helpful in finding apt quotations with which to state the mood of each of our twelve months.

During the months of labor required to bring the *Almanac* into creation, Lady Medea fell in and then out of love with her fellow Almanackist, Lemuel Pegg. This sequence of emotional events was inevitable, for Lemuel Pegg is, of course, that same Lemuel Pegg who is internationally known as "America's foremost life's loser."

Mr. Pegg's heart's loss was the *Almanac*'s gain, for his setback in love, combined with a peculiarly odious experience with the Internal Revenue Service, suffused his work with a sense of defeat and despair that he has seldom equaled in his lifelong struggle to convey to the world some feeling of what futility can be at its apex.

Perhaps the most beloved of our creative spirits is the frequently arrested Doctor Peregrine ("Doc") Dock, child psychologist, pediatrician, mass demonstrator and author of many manuals on how to survive after the baby comes. Doctor Dock, or "Doc" as he prefers to be called, is responsible for much that is finest in the *Almanac* about bestiality in human relationships, and particularly those relationships that involve children.

No work of this size could hope to succeed without a Plagiarist, of course, and the *Almanac,* fortunately, has one of the best. We cannot name him, as he is not above suing even himself for slander, but we can salute him by referring to him as—in capital letters—The Plagiarist. The public will find his touch everywhere in the *Almanac.*

Much of the material dealing with vacations, rich living, foreign pleasures, voluptuous hours and other aspects of the culture of hedonism is the work of the distinguished and able senior Senator from the now sunken State of Massagravy, Merle Survine. Senator Survine has also given us the fruit of his wisdom about Washington, D.C., and politics. And a rich compote it is.

The Senator's home state, Massagravy, it will be recalled, sank in the late 1950s under the weight of Federally financed highways, dams, military bases, shipyards, power plants, armament factories and penitentiaries that

Senator Survine had secured for it during his twenty-year struggle, as chairman of the Appropriations Committee, against excessive Federal spending. Massagravy finally buckled under the weight of a new Veterans' Administration hospital and slid to rest under three hundred feet of water on the continental shelf, leaving Senator Survine with little to do these past twenty-five years except improve his knowledge of Washington and politics.

Finally, there is our *sine quo non*—the man who provides the *Almanac* with the royal touch. He is the last surviving member of the Royal House of Stuart, which ruled England throughout the seventeenth century and eventually gave way—illegally, the Stuarts said—to the Hanovers. Now, abusively denounced by many as a fraud, Tom Stuart, who styles himself The New Old Pretender, maintains his serenity with regal elegance while waiting for the day when he will be summoned home to become the rightful King of England.

Without the gracious assistance of The New Old Pretender, the *Almanac* would have been helpless to resolve the many delicate questions of protocol, fishing, compost and sexual normalities that inevitably arise in a work of this nature.

A final word in explanation of our title. Having resolved to pool their wherewithal to produce the *Almanac,* most of these distinguished women and men had no doubt about what it should be called. "Poor Richard's Almanac," Senator Survine suggested at that first meeting.

Discussion was brief. Lady Medea noted that the name was not very original and made no sense at all, but said she thought this weighed in its favor. The Plagiarist agreed warmly. The public commonly waited twenty to thirty years before purchasing original works, he noted, and by that time—say, the year A.D. 2001 or 2011—income tax rates would probably be so high once again that it would be disastrous to have a financial interest in a book that was making money.

It was agreed immediately then that they would call it "Poor Richard's Almanac." In writing the title for the printer, however, The New Old Pretender, whose spelling is not the best, spelled "Richard" with the letters R-U-S-S-E-L-L. The printer set the title as *Poor Russell's Almanac.*

Even The Plagiarist liked it immediately. "It shows we've got a little originality," he said, "but not enough to scare anybody away."

JANUARY

ONE SNOW in a winter is happiness. Two snows are too many. Three snows are a penance visited upon cities that are unjust. Wise is the man who goes to Yucatan after the first snow for he shall escape the ravages of dipsomania, self-pity and misanthropy, and his shoes shall not be ruined.

JANUARY

...... 1 ......

This is a day of headache for many. There will also be football; much, much football. Because of the volume of the football, you are in no mood for getting acquainted with your *Almanac* today and are unlikely to be tomorrow. The following day will be Monday. Your *Almanac* despises Monday and will be in no mood to get acquainted with anybody. Therefore, put the *Almanac* aside until the new year is firmly entrenched and resume reading on January 4.

JANUARY

...... 4 ......

As the holidays recede, it is time once again to put gaiety, depression and irrationality behind us. When we become more civilized, January 4 may become known traditionally as the Day of the Renewal of Thought, for on this day we customarily turn once again to our minds for strength and sustenance, and to taste the rare pleasures of reason.

It was one of those terrible moments of truth. According to the newspaper, the New York Stock Exchange had conferred a Vice-Presidency upon John R. Bermingham, who was, the paper went on, "its head data processing man."

On any other day the eye would have glided defensively over the print and passed on to "Consumer Credit Climbs in Month," but on this particular day some still active recess of the brain cried, "Stop!" and the obedient eye stopped and focused clearly on the words "head data processing man."

Curiosity, awakened by the eye's abnormally long pause, sat up grumpily and asked, "What is a data processing man?" There was no answer, so Curiosity flipped the switch on the squawk box and announced that he wanted a conference right away.

"Oh boy," said Conscience to Torpor as they trudged into the board room, "it's going to be one of those days."

"Give me everything you have on file under 'data processing man,'" Curiosity demanded of Memory.

Memory riffled nervously through an extremely slender folder. "Well," said Memory, "I'm afraid there isn't much. Eye has been reading 'data processing' for several years now, but nobody has bothered to find out what data processing is."

The feminine member of the board, Intuition, interrupted to say that she had had the impression for a long time that data processing was an extremely vital kind of work that had become widespread because of the growing use of computers.

"You had an impression!" Curiosity sneered. "Don't you know that when you get an impression around here you're supposed to send me a memo so we can go to work and learn something about the world we're trying to think in?"

The always gallant Imagination intervened to draw the fire from poor Intuition. "Chief," said Imagination, "I think we can solve this by imagining this fellow Bermingham at work. I see Bermingham sitting in front of a huge computer. Tubes glowing. Very sinister. See the picture? The computer hums and grinds out a datum. Bermingham holds it up in the light, matches it with another datum already on his desk. 'Ah, ha!' says Bermingham, 'there's something peculiar here.' He picks up a phone and barks a command: 'Have the processing room ready in fifteen minutes. I'm coming in with two very acute data.' "

Imagination's voice trailed off under Sobriety's look of cold fury. "This is a fine way to run a brain," said Sobriety. "Doesn't anybody here even know what a datum looks like?"

There was a long silence.

"Let's forget it and play trivia," said Habit. "Who was the leader of the Thug murder cult in *Gunga Din?*"

"Eduardo Ciannelli!" cried Memory.

"What was the name of Bob Crosby's band?" asked Frivolity.

"The Bobcats!" shouted Habit.

"Who was Alfred M. Landon's running mate in 1936?"

"Frank Knox!" screamed a chorus in reply.

Conscience pounded the ganglia for attention, and when he had it he made a long speech. He said the team should be ashamed of itself. He called the board's attention to the sorry state of the world. Men had been processing data for years, he pointed out, yet not a single member of the team had had the initiative to find out what a datum looked like or what exciting new promises for mankind were involved in the new techniques of processing one.

It was a small point, admittedly, he went on; but it was indicative of the brain's general state of lethargy. Did the brain really believe it more important to know that Eduardo Ciannelli had played the chief apostle of Thuggee than to know how the real world was dealing with all the data that would surely hobble the march of progress unless they were competently processed?

"Frankly," he concluded, "I do not see how I can be expected to weigh the great issues of our time when not a single member of the board has even bothered to answer such a simple question as how a man processes data."

Guilt had already pulled a very long face, and at the far end of the table Rationalization was saying, "If data processors are so smart, let's see Bermingham tell us the name of Jack Armstrong's high school."

"Let's think about flying to France this summer," said Impulse.

"That reminds me of that girl in Paris," said Memory. "When was it now? 1949? No . . ."

Two aspirins, placed in the fuel system during Conscience's long harangue, began to take effect and Curiosity drowsed off.

"Do you know," Deduction muttered as the group filed out, "this place gets dumber every day."

....

MISERY, SECURITY AND HAPPINESS (1)

Misery is when you arrive home late at night after a five-hundred-mile drive and discover the whiskey cabinet is empty and the liquor stores have all closed five minutes ago.

Security is a suntan in February.

Happiness is your dentist's verdict that $10,000 worth of bridgework will save your originals for another two years.

JANUARY
····· 9 ·····

On this day in 1793 François Blanchard made the first balloon flight ever to transport a Presidential order. Blanchard rose from Philadelphia at 10:10 A.M. President Washington, before ascent, had handed him an order "to all to whom these presents shall come" directing that Blanchard be allowed "to descend in such places as circumstances may render most convenient." Forty-five minutes later circumstances rendered it most convenient for Blanchard to descend at Cooper's Ferry, New Jersey. It was a historic moment in the Presidency.

Richard M. Nixon was born on this day in 1913. Dining out would be an appropriate way to celebrate either event.

The blackout began several years ago in expensive restaurants catering to the clientele that takes other men's wives to lunch, but it has now spread to run-of-the-mill houses specializing in minute steaks and meatballs. All over the country, restaurant owners are snatching the light bulbs and replacing them with two-and-a-half-watt candle flickers. It is like eating under blankets.

All these darkened restaurants are fitted out by the same decorator. He is in love with dungeons and English pubs. The style he has evolved might be called pub-dungeon. He fills the room with black tables, black beams and black pictures, then turns off the lights and scatters swords, pikes, iron maidens and pewter plates about the room. Such light as there is comes from the dark red table cloths. This red has a sinister quality, as though filched from a dying sunset in the hills of Bram Stoker's Transylvania.

You arrive at the restaurant with mouth set for a quick $10 hamburger patty. A man in black, a white face in a Stygian mist, guides you past pikes, swords, halberds and pewter to a table, then disappears. Another face looms from the dark. Something that has lost its way en route to a seance? Not at all. It is the waiter.

The waiter wants to "take your drink orders." The innocents who do not want to precede their ground beef with booze will tell the waiter so. This is a serious mistake. American restaurants today despise temperance in all its forms. They regard the sale of meals as a cover for the saloon business. Anyone who does not want to tipple leaves the waiter bored. He vanishes in the dark, perhaps to place your name on a list of persons to receive ptomaine culture in their soup, and you wait and wait and wait.

If you wait long enough, the waiter will eventually return with a menu. You are, after all, occupying space that could be more profitably occupied by a drinking guest. Many persons tire of waiting, however, become angry about being ignored, and rise to search for the man in charge. This is an extremely serious mistake.

In 1977 in Cincinnati, one B. J. Dutton left his wife at a table to go in search of the captain, lost his bearings in the dark and crashed into a wall decorated with halberds and pikes. A pike fell from the wall and struck Dutton's foot, shearing off the tip of his shoe and amputating two toes.

In the ensuing uproar Dutton was mistaken for the headwaiter by an outraged nondrinker, who had been waiting fifty-five minutes for a menu, and was severely beaten with a pewter platter.

Dutton's wife, meanwhile, was unaware of her husband's problem. Another diner, who had been drifting about in the dark looking for the table at which he had left his secretary, mistook Dutton's vacant chair for his own and sat down beside Mrs. Dutton. She assumed naturally—it being too dark to see much—that he was Mr. Dutton returned from administering a severe reprimand to the headwaiter.

Mrs. Dutton almost immediately became puzzled, however, by the unusually zealous attention that her companion began paying her, and when he leaned into her ear and whispered, "Let's not go back to the office. Let's go to your place," she became curious.

"Is that you, B.J.?" she asked.

"Isn't this Elvira?" the man inquired.

"What have you done with my husband?" Mrs. Dutton screamed.

"I'm over here, darling!" cried B.J. from deep in the darkness. "I'm looking for my toes!"

The headwaiter arrived with searchlight and quite firmly ordered both Duttons to leave. "You are not fit to dine out American style," he told them.

Wise nondrinkers who insist on dining out American style say, "Bloody Marys" when the waiter calls for their drink orders. Poured on the table cloth, they leave no discernible stain. That is probably why the table cloths are always red.

....

The time may be near when refusal to answer the telephone is no longer a legitimate exercise of freedom from communication, but a punishable misdemeanor, like disturbing the peace.

JANUARY
..... 13 .....

Today is the 138th anniversary of the birth of Horatio Alger.

Mort and Jack, old friends who had done well since their last meeting many years ago, met by chance one day in the lobby of the most expensive hotel imaginable. They clasped hands and went into the bar to cultivate their relationship.

"Great to see you again, Mort," said Jack. "I can't promise you much in the way of service here today. My regular bartender is off."

"Just like my cook," said Mort. "Always taking the day off when I need her most. Say, you wouldn't mind if I phoned my lawyer and asked him to join us, would you?"

"Of course not. I wonder if he knows my lawyer. As a matter of fact, I'm expecting a call from my doctor. My yard man fell into the hedge clippers yesterday and I wanted my doctor to take a look at him."

"Gee," said Mort, "it sounds like you might have troubles there. Can I put you in touch with my insurance man?"

"Thanks, Mort," said Jack, "but I've got my secretary trying to get in touch with my own insurance man right now. But you're looking a little flabby, fellow. Why don't I introduce you to my masseur?"

"That's decent of you, Jack," said Mort, "but my tax man made me drop my own masseur three months ago. He doesn't think I can claim a medical deduction for massage."

The two men fell silent. Then, suddenly, Jack blurted, "I've got a tax man, too."

"I've got a broker," Mort replied.

"So who hasn't got a broker?" Jack retorted. "I've got an agent."

"I've got an agent and a business manager," Mort said. "And what's more, I've got an estate-management consultant."

"Look," said Jack, "this is silly, isn't it? What are we trying to prove, anyhow?"

"It's crazy," Mort agreed. "It's sick. Let's cut it out, huh?, and talk about old times."

"I've got a barber," said Jack.

"Jack, Jack! What's wrong with us?"

"It's this whole crazy society, Mort. We've got to fight it. We've got to be big enough to admit to ourselves, to say right out loud: 'It doesn't matter that I've got a regular bartender, a yard man, a cook, a lawyer, a doctor, an insurance man, a secretary, a masseur, a tax man, a broker, an agent, a business manager, an estate-management consultant and a barber.' All those people were acquired. They aren't really us, Mort. Let's talk about the real us."

"I've got a tailor," said Mort.

"I've got a tailor, too," said Jack. "And what's more, buddy, I've got a decorator."

"I've had a decorator for years," Mort snarled, "and now I've got a guitar teacher."

"Ha! Is that all! I've got a shirtmaker and a caterer!"

"Who hasn't!" shouted Mort. "I've got a nanny for the children."

"I've got an English nanny," said Jack.

"You need one," said Mort. "You need an analyst, too."

"I've got an analyst," said Jack.

"Big deal!" said Mort. "Anybody can have an analyst, but I want to tell you something, Jack baby. I've got a guru."

At this Jack sagged in his chair and seemed to become physically smaller. During the long silence that fell between them, cries of "I've got a tailor!" and "Oh yeah? Well I've got a yard man!" could be heard from the other tables in the room.

At last, grinning in triumph, Mort said, "You don't have a guru, do you, Jack?"

"I admit it," Jack whispered. "I don't have a guru, Mort, but do me a big favor for old times' sake, would you, pal? Don't mention it to anybody?"

"I won't even tell my secretary," Mort said.

"You were always a swell guy, Mort."

"We're sick, Jack, sick. We've got to put all this craziness behind us and get down to the real essential us."

"You're so right, Mort. I've got a chiropodist."

"I've got a . . ."

....

What makes it possible for "the beautiful people" to winter in Martinique, toboggan at St. Moritz and enjoy the gloriously unbuttoned gaiety of Klosters? The answer is winter-soluble children.

When people contemplate a winter vacation they immediately run head-on into the question, "What are we going to do with the children?" They can arrange to fly now, pay later, and ski now, pay later, but what will they do with the children?

Beautiful people never have this problem. Their children go into suspension with the first frost and stay that way until their parents come back to open the flower shows.

JANUARY

..... 27 .....

Mozart's 226th Birthday

The all-purpose opera, composed during a coma induced by a Saturday-afternoon broadcast of *Die Walküre,* or perhaps *La Bolognarria di Siviglia:*

As the curtain rises, we hear the ghostly "Schwamp-musik" sung by the Frog Maidens of the Danube as they lament the fate which compels them to stand guard over the swampy approaches to the underwater summer palace of the Duke of Palermo. Twenty fathoms down, there are distant sounds of rejoicing from the Duke's household as the chorus celebrates the birth of twins, Giulietta and Joachim, to the happy ducal couple.

As the Duke and his faithful valet, Mazeppa, sing the

joyous duet, "Nicht ein, aber zwei," the Frog Maidens are approached by a mysterious gypsy fortune teller who offers to tell their fortunes. Singing the menacing "Song of the Kidnapadors," the gypsy crone predicts that the Frog Maidens will immediately be transformed into Wagnerian sopranos unless they give her an aqualung and the key to the palace door.

Reluctantly, the Frog Maidens obey, pleading in the beautiful chorus, "Taken sie nicht both kinder, alte crone," for the gypsy to leave one baby for the Duke. The gypsy agrees ("Ja, ja, ein für mir und uno per duco") as the curtain falls on Act I.

In Act II, the plot comes to a halt while Wotan and Thor sing the immortal "Lebensraumenlungenlied" ("Where is the life that once we led?"). A fifty-minute intermission follows to allow the audience to have prescriptions filled.

Act III opens with a gay wedding reception in Cadiz. Joachim, now a handsome young tenor disguised as a wastrel cavalier, is searching for his long-lost sister, Giulietta, who was kidnapped many years ago by the gypsies. Accompanied by his father's faithful valet, Mazeppa, Joachim observes the joyous wedding celebration, then pours out his heart to the faithful valet in the beautiful "Papa non e longo per questo mondo" ("I travel the world to reunite Giulietta with father before he dies").

Mazeppa's aria, "Est-ce-que je ne le sais pas bien?" ("You're telling me!") draws the attention of the ravishing but fatally ill courtesan, Rosa Maria, who is the life of the wedding party. Flirting with the downcast Joachim, she sings the enchanting "Warum So Glum?" ("Cheer Up!") as Joachim blushes with boyish embarrassment. It is soon obvious, however, that he is smitten, for he strides to the center of the wedding party and leads the chorus in the ever rousing "La Hababeera," and all join in hoisting huge tankards of Cadiz ale as the curtain falls on Act III.

Word that Joachim's search for Giulietta has foundered in Cadiz, while he sings "La Hababeera" nightly to the voluptuous tubercular Rosa Maria, has reached the dying Duke of Palermo during the intermission. In the opening scene of Act IV the Duke, arriving in Cadiz, begs Rosa Maria to give up his son, move her household to Paris and set Joachim free. Sobbing and coughing, Rosa Maria agrees to go in the pathetic aria, "En France on dit 'Oui, oui' " ("I love Paris in the autumn when it drizzles"). The curtain falls.

In Scene II Wotan goes mad, followed closely by Thor.

In Scene III Joachim learns that Rosa Maria has left Cadiz. Furious with his father, he tells him he loves Rosa Maria ("Rosa Maria, I love you") and announces that he is going to Paris to dine with a statue who, he has reason to believe, knows Giulietta's whereabouts.

As Joachim storms out, the Duke sings the murderous aria, "Was gibt mit statues ge-meeten?" ("That a son of mine should expect me to believe that cock-and-bull story!").

In Act V the Duke, believing that Joachim has really come to Paris to meet Rosa Maria, arrives at the banqueting hall early and instructs his faithful valet, Mazeppa, to put poison in the wine to be given Joachim's guest. Mazeppa, who has gone mad, agrees.

The statue arrives before Joachim and to wet its whistle ("Ach, ich habe ein thirst!") drinks the poisoned wine. The statue is dying when Joachim arrives. "Mort! Mort!" it screams. "I'm not Mort," sings Joachim, "I'm Joachim" ("Non sono Mortone, ich bin Joachim!"). "And I," sings the statue, "am your long-lost sister, Giulietta." She dies.

Learning that he has murdered his own daughter, the Duke kills himself. Joachim, crazed by the tragedy, curses Wotan and Thor ("Basta, Wotane! Basta, Thorone!").

Infuriated, Wotan and Thor turn Joachim into a Frog Maiden as the dying Rosa Maria sings the timeless "O Salve Mio" ("Bring Me Some Salve"). Curtain.

....

ENGLISH (1)

English is a language in which grown people see nothing peculiar about telling a child, "Sit down and sit up."

JANUARY

⸺ 30 ⸺

On this day in 1649, King Charles I of England was beheaded in London. Democracy was on the march.

⸺⸺⸺

EXCERPTS FROM A ROYAL DIARY

They told me this morning I was the new King. "That's great!" I said. "I'll go right upstairs and tell Lucinda she's a Queen." "Better not," said the Prime Minister's Second Secretary. "As she is a commoner it is quite impossible for her to become Queen." I was furious. Why do they send me only the Prime Minister's Second Secretary to break such news? "Kings aren't what they used to be, your royal whatever-it-is," the fellow said. Insolent lout.

Lucinda was furious for the second day running. Yesterday the assistant to the Assistant Equerry told her it was "quite impossible" for her to attend the matinee at the Essex Road Odeon on the spur of the moment. Today she is told she must open a new eel-pickling plant. Poor girl! Royalty goes hard with her. But of course she is only a commoner.

I am ridiculed in the press today for walking barefoot last night in the palace garden. Apparently I was photographed by an American who was having dinner in that restaurant on top of the London Hilton looking right down into the palace. "If you go out of the palace again in inappropriate attire," the Assistant Royal Wardrobe Master warned me, "I shall tell the Prime Minister's executive secretary, who may very well reduce your living allowance."

The commotion about what title to give Lucinda rages in press and Parliament. The Socialist left wing insists upon "The Commoner Woman," which prompted Lucinda to ask me just now, "Commoner than who?" *"Whom,* dear," I replied. "The correct form is 'commoner than *whom.'* Won't you ever learn to speak my English?" Later I wondered if it really was "commoner than whom" and asked the Palace Information Office if it would check with a good grammarian. "I haven't time for such piffle," said the fellow at the desk. "Do you know who I am?" I asked. "No," he said, "and as I happen to be a civil servant, I have no reason to care."

I am forbidden to go to the football games. Too unregal, they say. "Take up polo," they suggest. "It's more kinglike."

What a depressing day. The Minister for Tourism has been bullying me about not making more frequent appearances on the palace balcony. It seems the tourists are complaining that I do not come to the balcony often enough for their taste. The Minister threatened to tell the Prime Minister I am failing in my obligation to promote tourism and help increase sales of snapshot film. I told him I would think it over. He asked if I didn't know that it was a breach of the Constitution for a King to think, and handed me a schedule of hourly balcony appearances which, he said, is already being posted in all hotel lobbies.

Lucinda opened a slag heap in Wales today.

I am now ridiculed in the papers for taking polo lessons on a heavily sedated horse. Have just telephoned the Ministry of Information asking why I must be subjected to such abuse, especially as I have no interest in either polo or horses. "Without you to ridicule," the clerk explained, "the press might turn its attention to the government."

Lucinda refused to open a batch of new train coaches today unless she could invite Elizabeth Taylor to the palace for dinner some evening. She was told this was "quite impossible" since Liz is such a public advocate of divorce, but a showing of the new Disney film can be arranged for her in the privacy of the palace.

I now ride out through the palace gates twice daily in a horse-drawn coach so that the tourists may exercise their cameras more fully. The Deputy Equerry says I must stop waving my crown like an American politician. The royal coach creates a terrible nuisance with the traffic, being so slow; today I was soundly abused by some stalled truck drivers who said they would like to encounter me aboard my polo pony on a main highway some day.

Today I was taken to Parliament, handed a speech written by the Prime Minister and told to read it to the assembled Lords and Commons. As it was scarcely literate, I was so embarrassed that upon finishing I said, "And now I would like to say a few words of my own." I was seized by the police, gagged and carried away. "Am I to be dethroned?" I inquired. "Do you take me for a fool?" the Prime Minister replied. "Where do you think we'd ever find another king?"

While opening a new airplane today, Lucinda drew a revolver on the pilot and ordered him to fly her to Paris, where she has gone into exile at the Ritz. My bodyguard has been doubled.

JUGLIPIDITY

The English language is suffering from a word shortage. This is because the world changes so fast nowadays that word makers cannot produce new words fast enough to keep up with all the new things that are happening.

For example, the Volkswagen has been with us for thirty-five years, but we still do not have a good word to describe the peculiar state of mind which the Volkswagen induces in its driver. Without such a word, other drivers have no effective way of dealing with the Volkswagen driver as he weaves in and out of heavy traffic, feeling dangerously like a broken-field runner on an asphalt gridiron.

All you can do when you catch one of these people at a red light is lean out the window and say, "You're suffering from lethal delusions of mobility," or something equally cumbersome. The word we need here is, obviously "miniphoria," a descriptive noun suggesting the odd euphoria that comes over people hunched in miniature machines. When you catch a Volkswagen driver at the light, you simply lean out the window and roar, "You stupid miniphoriac!" and the world becomes a satisfying place again.

Another modern condition for which there is no adequate word is the appearance of women walking along the street in tightly fitting trousers, slacks or jeans. Everyone has seen this modern spectacle, but at present dozens of imprecise words are needed to discuss it. Words like "rippling," "quivering," "bulging," "ballooning," etc.

What we need is a single noun that succinctly sums up the condition. Such a word might be "juglipidity." With "juglipidity," the spectacle will no longer leave us speechless. Seeing one of these poor creatures in public, we will only have to say,

"That poor woman's juglipidity is acute," and the situation will be satisfactorily disposed of.

We also need a word for the modern crime of robbery by machine. In the typical mechanized robbery, the victim puts fifty cents into a soda-pop vending machine. The machine seizes the money, drops it into a metal loot box, and refuses to come across with the soda pop.

The victim is baffled. If he had been robbed by a man with a gun, he would know what to do. He would go to the police, report the commission of a felony and, after the bandit had been caught, testify in court to put the wretch behind bars.

Against a felonious machine, there is no apparent recourse. What is the word for this offense that has been committed? What are the victim's rights once he has futilely punched the coin-return lever a few times? Is it permissible to kick the machine? Should it be turned over to the police?

If there were a familiar word for this all-too-familiar modern crime, the victim could act with reason. The word we need is "slottery," a noun meaning "robbery by a coin-vending machine."

Give crime its proper name and man can deal with it. When the machine grabs his fifteen cents, the victim, no longer faced with an indefinable situation, will cry, "Ah ha! So slottery's your game, eh?" He will then feel perfectly justified in attacking the thief with a jack handle, recovering his money from the loot box and stuffing the machine's slots with chewing gum.

············

The cigarette users of the world form a dark brotherhood that, like the Mafia, hates a defector. Upon learning that a member is trying to break the habit, they devise a thousand subtle and tortuous ways to make his life miserable until he comes back to smoke. Cigarette smokers shrug off the health threat. "Everyone," they say, "must die." They have learned to contemplate the early grave with equanimity, but they hate to think of leaving their friends behind.

FEBRUARY

WHAT! Both Monday and February can occur on the same day?

FEBRUARY

...... 1 ......

With the onset of February the year reaches its hour of letdown, a time when life seems slightly leaden, the sunshine—when there is any—a frozen glint off cold metal, and the chill that sits deep in the marrow more than the spirit can bear. It is a time for rummaging in memory's attic among the stored-up moments from the past that we have put away to help us survive just such a season as this. Ah, yes, once it was summer . . . Once we crossed blue warm seas and came to rest in a magic city of campaniles and Byzantine domes where orchestras played in the sunlight . . . Ah, summer long ago! . . . Ah, Venice . . .

It was humiliating walking into St. Mark's Square the first time. This was five days ago. There were fifty thousand people in that Square and this man in the light gray suit, Panama hat and sunglasses, ignoring the other 49,999, walked right up and said, "Come see the glass factory." In English yet.

Now everybody should undoubtedly see a glass factory before he dies, but that is not the point. The point is that nobody who is a tourist wants to be recognized as a tourist, and when a Venetian asks you to come see a glass factory it means you have "tourist" written all over you.

When he speaks in English, it means he has identified you as an American tourist. (Italians have long since learned not to trifle with British tourists; British tourists are notoriously testy with Italians and may reply with a punch to the jaw if urged too eagerly to come see the glass factory.)

The British, of course, are different from all other tourists. They enjoy being British in other people's countries, whereas all other tourists want to be mistaken for the natives. Italy is filled with Germans, huddling Teutonically over beer in terror of being recognized as German tourists, and with Americans starved for hamburger but determined not to look like Americans by ordering it.

Anyhow, it is an insufferable humiliation when the man in the gray suit, Panama hat and sunglasses picks you out of the crowd of fifty thousand for the glass factory tour. You retreat to a dark place and brood.

"Is it so obvious," you ask a beautiful woman at the bar, "that I am an American tourist?"

"How would you like to see my uncle's glass factory?" she replies.

By next day things are better. You have mailed the camera home and bought an electric-blue suit, a pair of basketweave shoes and smoked glasses. Feeling intensely Italian, you wander into the Square whistling a Neapolitan street song.

Suddenly, burrowing straight through the mob and homing in on radar comes the man in the light gray suit, Panama hat and smoked glasses. "Come see the glass factory," he implores.

The hotel porter is sympathetic. "Perhaps if the signor had an Italian haircut and tried walking with more snap in his step instead of the American slouch."

Why not? Time is running out in Venice, and something has to be done if one is to see the cathedral, the Palace of the Doges and the Tintorettos without having the pleasure spoiled by feeling like a despicable tourist.

And so, on the third day, stripped of the telltale camera, glistening in electric-blue suit, eyes shaded behind smoked glasses, sideburns shaved to knife points, basketweave shoes tripping along in the Italian quickstep, you cross the Square and mount the cathedral steps.

That hand on your elbow. How strangely familiar it feels. "Come see the glass factory," says the voice of the light gray suit, the Panama hat and the sunglasses.

You sit in dark rooms, hating Venetian glass and Panama hats, feeling the magic of Venice evaporate.

By the fourth night it is only a question of rescuing something from the trip. Venice is a city of romance—of gondolas, canals and olive-skinned contessas with languorous eyes. And so under cover of night, wearing a rented pencil-thin mustache below the smoked glasses, you place a beautiful contessa in a gondola and instruct the gondolier to sing sweetly.

The spell of the Venetian night is enchanting as the gondola glides through a labyrinth of narrow-bridged canals presenting unending vistas of discarded bleach bottles, rotting tomatoes, used celery stalks and drowned rats, all drifting romantically on the current.

Sighs rise from the gondola. Here and there along the canals, gay lights denote an outdoor restaurant where the diners wave happily as you drift along on the effluvium. Ahead there is a small bridge of infinite grace.

Silhouetted figures wave happily. But what is this?

"Look," cries the ecstatic contessa in flawless Italian. "There is a charming man in a light gray suit, Panama hat and sunglasses."

From up on the bridge he leans over, cups hands to mouth and cries in flawless English, "Come see the glass factory!"

And the contessa replies in a voice full of triumph: "Where else would I be taking him?"

FEBRUARY

⋯⋯ 6 ⋯⋯

Every even-numbered year in America is an election year and this year is no exception. Election campaigns now last at least a full year and may soon go on forever. If you doubt it, shovel into a ten-foot snow drift and chances are that, five feet down, you will come across a politician making typical American noises.

Following are some translations into English from that strange tongue, Politigabble:

"My fellow Americans"—"Anybody who switches to the channel showing the movie is unpatriotic."

"It's wonderful to be back in the American heartland"—"What's the name of this dump?"

"Let's look at the record"—"Let's not."

"Peace with honor"—"War."

"Never has the threat to democratic government been more grave . . ."—"My polls show I am likely to get beaten."

"Let us never heed extremists from both sides"—"What's wrong with taking a little money from the oil industry?"

"Without regard to race, creed or color"—"Ho hum."

"Many people have asked me to clarify my position on Ameri-

can policy toward subsidies for the rectified juice industry"—
"My ghost writer thinks there's some political mileage in
this, so I agreed to try it."

*"Let us remember that these wonderful young people are our
citizens of tomorrow"*—"At present, however, they are still
just punks."

*"On the way over here this afternoon a little girl came up to
me and said . . ."*—"This isn't really true, of course, but
my television adviser says it is good for my image to tell
absurd anecdotes like this."

"I shall never stoop to smear and innuendo"—"The polls
show I have it won if I play it cool."

"Let us not judge a man by the way he cuts his hair"—"I
trust everyone has noticed that my opponent has not cut
his for more than a year."

*"My opponent's religion should not be an issue in this cam-
paign, and I will never heed the advice of those who are urging
me to make it an issue"*—"In case it has not been generally
observed here, I would like to point out that he adheres
to a minority sect with extremely odd views on transub-
stantiation."

"And standing there in that kibbutz, I said . . ."—"No
Arab, I."

*"My opponent has sought to sell himself as though he were
a powder for the relief of acid indigestion through the use of the
most expensive campaign of television huckstering in the history
of American government. This crass commercial cheapening of
public office is a vice in which I shall never indulge."*—"I am in
truly desperate need of funds to purchase television time."

"As Walter Bagehot once said of politics . . ."—"Will any intellectuals in the audience please note that I have a ghost writer who knows who Walter Bagehot is, and will tell me if I want to know?"

"The disgruntled young must learn to work effectively within the system for the reforms they so ardently desire"—"Do as I say, and in time you may be elected to public office to do as I don't, and have no intention of doing."

". . . and I pledge myself to the defense of the Constitution of the United States"—"Upon being elected, I shall immediately offer six amendments to the Constitution to do away with certain unconstitutional provisions now embedded in that document, and to make constitutional certain practices which it now, unfortunately, forbids."

"How wonderful it is to get away from Washington and be back here with the people!"—"At least it gives my liver that rest the doctor ordered."

"Now, I am going to be perfectly honest about this"—"Oh no, I'm not."

INTERCEPTED LETTERS

Dear H. B. Simms:

After considerable research I have established that you are the president of the Hildebrand Variable Lithograph Disseminating Society, and I am writing about a matter of the utmost gravity to your organization.

Eight months ago I bought a variable lithograph disseminator from your society and paid the full amount for it—$32.89

—three days after delivery. I have the canceled check for that amount. Notwithstanding, I have been dunned by an exceedingly nasty computer for the past seven months. This computer claims to represent your organization. Despite my sending it a dozen letters pointing out its error, it persists in stating that I still owe you the $32.89 that I paid you eight months ago.

The other day this machine sent me an abusive letter calling me a deadbeat and threatening to ruin my credit rating by the spreading of slander. I must warn you, H. B. Simms, that unless your computer stops threatening me, I intend to pay a nocturnal visit to its residence in Armonk, New York, and give it a severe thrashing with an ax, which I bought just yesterday for this specific purpose.

Lest you think this mere hollow bluster, be assured, sir, that I have just been released from a hospital for the criminally insane where I have been resting as a result of earlier antisocial activities with axes.

Sincerely yours,

FEBRUARY
⋯⋯ 12 ⋯⋯

Lincoln's Birthday

He seems surprisingly tall when seen silhouetted down an abandoned Washington street. Perhaps it is the stovepipe hat. He never walks the night streets without it. Once, he says, he took his nocturnal walk wearing a porkpie hat but felt like an anachronism.

"It was three days before I began to feel like Abe Lincoln again," he said, in that odd mountain accent of his. It is hard getting accustomed to Mr. Lincoln's own voice. Everyone wants him to sound like Raymond Massey or Henry Fonda.

One night when we were taking one of his favorite strolls, along Seventeenth Street at Farragut Square, a group of college students looking for pizza momentarily recognized him. "You're Abraham Lincoln," a student observed.

"Indeed I am," Mr. Lincoln replied. "If you are looking for pizza, I would propose Luigi's around on Nineteenth Street."

"That's not Lincoln," one of the students said.

"Some kind of nut," suggested his girl.

"Sounds like a hillbilly."

Mr. Lincoln always smiles at these encounters. Not sounding like Raymond Massey or Henry Fonda is the surest guarantee of his privacy, which he cherishes. He enjoys conversation if it is not about the past, and he likes ethnic jokes. Upon hearing a good one, he characteristically stops dead on the sidewalk and slaps his knee with delight.

One tries delicately to improve his taste. "The better class of people, Mr. President, no longer laughs at jokes of that sort."

"How's that?" is invariably his response. "Do you mean to say that you can't laugh at some of the people some of the time any more?"

He occasionally goes to his Memorial to look at the marble rendering of himself from a distance. "I used to come down here and have a good laugh at that thing," he says. "And then I read about myself in Carl Sandburg, and ever since, whenever I look at myself up there in tons of cold marble, I think, considering the kind of fellow Mr. Sandburg discovered me to be, the Union didn't really do right by me."

He laughs. It is his idea of a joke.

"I was never very good with jokes," he recalled one windy March night as we were walking around Dupont Circle looking at the younger class of people and their guitars. "Couldn't remember them. They'd pass in one ear and right out the other. Then I read Sandburg's biography and memorized all those wonderfully funny stories he says I used to tell. The trouble was, I couldn't rid myself of the habit of prefacing each one with the words, 'As Abraham Lincoln once said . . .'"

"Move along, Mac," a Dupont Circle policeman warned him, "before I run you in for impersonating a President."

"Did you really say once that you were going to find out what kind of whiskey Grant drank and order some for all your generals, Mr. President?"

"I doubt that there is anything to be gained by either party to this stroll in a discussion of the past."

This is the same answer he invariably gives if asked, "Was there an Ann Rutledge?" "Were you, as fashionably charged nowadays, really a racist?" "Did you truly write the Gettysburg Address on an envelope?"

Once, as we stood on the Capitol's west terrace at midnight looking down the Mall toward George Washington's obelisk, he explained his aversion to a reopening of the past. "A man," he said, "eventually likes to see the record on himself completed and know that everything is fixed and that his life is in order. I groan every time an archivist discovers another hitherto lost Brady portrait of me."

Sometimes he disappears inexplicably. Oh, not right there on the street while you are inspecting a dress shop window with him. Nothing like that. It is only that he is not *around* for weeks at a time.

"I wish you wouldn't ask me where I go during these lapses of mine," he requested once, as we were chatting over coffee in an all-night waffle house. "Suffice it to say that where I go is sufficient unto my purpose for going."

Discretion is always indicated with Mr. Lincoln, out of respect, but occasionally he enjoys being pressed. "And what would be your purpose in going, Mr. President?"

"To achieve nonexistence," he explained with unusual gravity. He explained: He was, from time to time, invited to the White House to confer with a President. He could not bear the thought of going there, for he knew that his presence would be used largely as an occasion for giving the news photographers an unusual photograph, and that after a few vacuous remarks with the sitting President he would be sedately shown back into the streets.

He does not object to being photographed with Presidents, but he is afraid that during the vacuous remarks which must inevitably follow he will blurt out some advice about what the host-President ought to be doing. "I am painfully familiar with the temptation," he said, "for I have seen it happen to better men than I. Once when I had George Washington in during 1862, the old fellow couldn't forbear telling everyone in earshot that my policy on *habeas corpus* was tyrannical and inimical to every principle for which he and his colleagues had fought."

"Shameful, Mr. President!"

"Oh no. George was perfectly right. That is always the worst part of it. The best thing is to say you can't come to the White House because you do not exist."

"And you disappear?"

"Not at all! According to a friend of mine at the Pentagon, I don't disappear. What I do is practice selective dis-existence."

When he pronounced that mouthful he slapped his knee in delight and spilled his coffee in his stovepipe hat, which he had set on the floor.

"I like a good laugh," Mr. Lincoln said. "That's why I try to make so many friends at the Pentagon."

Constant exposure to the shocked reports that America is a wild party may alarm the naïve, but the sensible person will eventually start wondering why he never receives an invitation. He may read these reports of the wild party that is America and tell himself that life is passing him by. He has heard all his life about the wild parties. First in the fraternity house, then in the barracks. Men who claimed to have attended these wild parties have inflamed his imagination. But when he went with these very men in search of bacchanalia, it always turned out to be beer and pretzels, and later in life, celery stuffed with cheese.

With age, he slowly accepted the drab truth: In the average city of three million people the number of wild parties held in the average year can be counted on the fingers of one hand. What is worse, these four or five wild parties are always attended by the same people—a handful of professional wild-party goers and five hundred magazine writers who are gathering material for articles on sex-drenched America.

FEBRUARY
⋯⋯ 14 ⋯⋯

Valentine's Day

"Will you be my valentine?" asked he.
"Forever," said she.

"I'm had!" said he.

"It's not bad," said she, "considering that henceforth we shall ever afterward live happily."

Next year he brought sweets in a heart-shaped box.

And a card reeking with arch sentiment for "the girl who darns my socks."

"At tender moments like this," he murmured, "wives customarily choose to break the news that the house will soon echo to baby's shoes."

She wept, for instead of a great deal of talk about shoes and socks, she yearned to be the valentine of the kind of man who would dine her on champagne and lox.

A year passed. "Guess what tomorrow is," she said.

Thus prompted, he rushed muttering to the drugstore. "Three-hundred-and-sixty-four days a year this woman cares for her rug more, but if on the fourteenth of February I forget to hand her a three-pound assortment of chocolate confection and a mass-produced affidavit of unceasing affection, she sees red."

In the fourth year of love he gave her a potted geranium, and in the fifth a limited edition of prints showing amorous antics in old Herculaneum.

"While I'm all for love," he said to a friend, "Valentine's Day gives me a pain in the cranium."

Next year at breakfast with the eggs she served him a card that said, "To me you're as thrilling as fissioning uranium."

Though he hated doggerel that didn't scan, being a

man with a fairly typical wife on his hands, he did what he knew he'd better do, and bought her a dozen roses and a card that said:

> *My love for you I send this day;*
> *Let thy heart be mine.*
> *Though these old feet be made of clay,*
> *They pine sorely to be thine.*

The next year he remembered a week ahead, for in the seventh year man, particularly if his scalp has begun to shed, may note that visions of his boss's secretary inevitably succeed such philosophical reflection as "All men end up dead."

"I will make a frank admission of my passion anonymously," he said, referring to the secretary, and bought a card, which read:

> *Intenser than a seething furnace,*
> *My love for you I'm breathing earnest.*
> *Your beauty coals the leaping fire;*
> *Spurn not, sweet stoker, thy unsleeping sigh-er.*

"You were going to remember all along!" cried his wife, who had discovered it in his wallet pocket on February eleventh. It being the seventh year of their living happily ever afterward, she was naturally sappily happy about still being able to be a valentine to a seething furnace, and when she asked, "Am I truly thy sweet stoker, oh leaping fire?'' he realized the real size of the prize he would possess in this woman if only, in the middle of every February, she would not campaign so hard for an inane card and take better care of his socks.

That night, in a seizure of guilty emotion, he finally dined her on champagne and lox.

But the eighth year rolled around, and on the evening of February 14, the mailman having delivered nothing more exciting than news of three new publishing miracles, they conversed.

"You forgot," said she.

"What?" asked he.

"Valentine," said she.

"Rot!" snarled he. "How long have I got to go on explaining of what I think valentines are a lot?"

Year nine. "Be mine," said the card he placed by her bed.

She turned red.

"Where's mine?" he said.

"I forgot," said she.

"I see."

"I think," said she, "that whoever is responsible for Valentine's Day just wanted to see that people did not live ever afterward happily."

"You forgot," said he, and attempted to cry, but gave it up as a bad try.

MISERY, SECURITY AND HAPPINESS (2)

Misery is when you are at a party and the loveliest woman in the room asks you to do the new mumbo-bumbo frogstep with her and you have to tell her that your rheumatism is killing you.

Security is a reserved parking space downtown.

Happiness is when somebody you know has kicked the cigarette habit and has been tormenting you for still smoking and you go into the washroom one day and catch him lighting up.

FEBRUARY

······ 22 ······

Washington's Birthday

Six of the wisest men in the world met in New York a few years ago to discuss man's chances of surviving in the kind of world that man is creating. They were optimistic. That optimism, issuing from men of wisdom, is still reassuring, and yet—

Well, these cards keep arriving in the mail. Everyone must know about these cards. They are usually filled with little holes which are arranged in patterns that make sense to computers, or they bear a long series of Arabic numerals which look crippled and arthritic. They always come accompanied by nasty warnings.

"Failure to produce this card on demand may result in your being publicly humiliated," they declare. Or, "This card must be kept on your body at all times." And, "Any attempt to correspond with us without enclosing the serial number on this card is a grave offense punishable by slow asphyxiation in a sealed room."

These cards raise the essential question in any discussion of man's chances for survival. The question is, what is this man whose survival we are talking about? Certainly the kind of organism that was called man two hundred years ago—the man, for example, whom his colleagues called George Washington—would find it hard to survive our card way of life.

The 1776 model George Washington would be unsafe if he tried to cross the boulevard on foot, much less to move two tons of metal into 60-mile-an-hour traffic, but that is only a small part of it. His more serious problem would be psychic. Surely he could not accept a life that compelled him to become a walking file cabinet. Even if he were able, after several years of psychotherapy, to make what is nowadays called a healthy adjustment by accepting the card life-style, he would cease altogether to be that man who was capable once of leading a tatterdemalion band of rebels into battle against his own government.

Imagine the eighteenth-century man, perhaps the highest form of humanity mankind ever reached, struggling to cope with a routine day in the last third of the twentieth century.

Upon waking, he is clubbed with a staccato of bad news from absolutely everywhere, which is emitted by a talking box. Between bursts of bad news about humanity and the cosmos, the box warns him that physical decay and social ruin yawn immediately ahead unless he protects himself with the correct purchases from the drugstore.

To reach his job he is mounted on wheels and moved at terrifying speeds while cudgeling masses crush his instep and pummel his kidney with elbow points. Instead of reporting for muscular exercise in airy fields, he is penned into a sealed room and bathed in artificial light and secondhand air. If in business, he may have to abuse his liver at lunch with quantities of alcohol. The telephone saws on his nerve endings. People furious about having been born demand his cards, his numbers.

At home in the evening he is swathed in layers of cacophony. The children have a box that screams, "Ee-yuh, ee-yuh, ee-yuh!" His wife has a box that lights up and shows men screaming about beer, gasoline, dandruff, foul breath, headache, reeking armpit. In this atmosphere he must do his day's accounting, perfecting the ledgers, balance sheets and files required by the Internal Revenue Service, for modern living is, except for the part that is noise, all business. The telephone jangles through the night. Machines ring him up to announce that he has won six bottles of carbonated soda water or a free dance lesson. Relatives call from the Yukon and the Pampas with the up-to-the-minute bad news.

The automatic garbage grinder grinds. The refrigerator hums. Fans whir. The furnace rumbles, or air conditioners purr. Fuses blow. The automatic laundry shakes the house. The blender whines. The night air quivers with the screams of neighbors approaching insanity. Day and night the house is pelted with printed matter smacking its print contentedly about the latest diseases, corruption, murders, royal visits, stock exchange fluctuations, floods, locusts, lynchings.

And day after day the cards arrive. "This card supersedes your old card." "Keep this card on your person at all times." "Failure to treat this card with the utmost respect will bring you under investigation by the Federal Government."

The creature that was man in 1750 would be only slightly less out of place than Brontosaurus in the present world. By any reasonable definition, he is already extinct. What has evolved is a creature thicker in the pot, longer in the shank, weaker in the back, softer in hand and foot and more easily winded than his predecessor.

These are only minor mutations. The important one is the development of steel-wire nerves. This creature will probably not survive either, but something metallic and tranquilized that can be called man will probably come along as the world continues to improve.

ENGLISH (2)

English may be the only language in the world in which a Mafia don can "sit in" on a "sitdown," then go home and tell his wife he has been "sitting around" all day.

FEBRUARY

⸺ 29 ⸺

This rarest of days, when it occurs, reminds us that once, in a charming old time, a charming old myth that was never taken seriously had it that Leap Year was a time when certain courting roles were reversed between male and female, and woman might go freely in pursuit of a mate. Betty Friedan, you have lifted the scales from our eyes and equalized the distribution of dishpan hands.

REFLECTIONS UPON WASHING THE DISHES

This, then, is what they mean when they grouse about sexism? These tedious plates with tiny chunks of grease bonded to the pattern, this splattered lamb fat congealing on my trousers. No wonder they wear those dreary aprons. Still, it's mindless work. Something to be said for that. Leaves you time to think. About?

That girl having the martini today at lunch at the Black Bird Café. Girls having martinis at lunch, pretty ones. Makes you wonder who runs the office in the afternoon nowadays, what with their bosses all coming back from lunch fried on three and four martinis.

That's probably what they mean by male chauvinism. Having to go on working after their martinis, while the boss is sleeping his off on the couch in his office, door closed, can't be interrupted, in conference.

What am I supposed to do with the leftover Brussels sprouts?

The trouble with America today is. Isn't that what is called a portentous phrase? No. Banal phrase. Washing dishes brings out the portentous banality in a man's phrases. Coffee grounds went in my pants cuff. They say they make good mulch.

The trouble with America today is that people who have power never wash the dishes. If Nixon had washed the dishes every night, or Congress had washed the dishes, there would not have been so much upheaval, unrest, student discontent, hair, law and order, John Mitchell, Black Panthers, Ché, Ike, good old days.

Take this electric dishwashing machine right here. What good is it? If you've got to rub the bonded grease chunks off the plates, scrape the hardened milk ring off the glasses and sandpaper the pots before you can put them into the dishwasher with any hope of having them come out clean, what good is the dishwasher?

No good! No good at all!

Must be careful of excessively strong judgments. Grave weakness of mine. Modify, modify! Always modify.

Still, not much good. Dishwasher's not much good. Not much improvement over old-fashioned Brand X dishpan-washing techniques just like Mother used to make. Still, women are grateful for it. Drive you up the wall to buy them a dishwasher, then figure you'll gloat, I guess, if they complain about it not being much good. Poor things.

Trouble is people who have power never wash the dishes. Suppose Reagan had to bathe in this steaming mess of grease, coffee grounds, salad oil every night. He would soon get on the phone to some Bill or Bob he knows, millionaire, made it all in dishwashers.

"You know what, Bill or Bob?" Reagan would say. "The automatic dishwasher isn't much better than the old-fashioned dishpan. Why don't you make one that really washes the dishes automatically?"

And Bill or Bob would say, "No kidding? Not much good, eh? You don't say, Mr. President?" Because Bill or Bob would never have washed dishes either. Too rich, too much power, so wouldn't know that their own machine wasn't much good.

My hand!

Scalded! Scalded!

And nobody even cares! They're still sitting in there

watching that stupid television set, playing it so loud they can't even hear me scream.

That's the trouble with America today. People who have power to make things happen don't do things that people do, so they don't know what needs to happen. Take railroads. If Presidents had to ride the railroad to Santa Barbara, California, like people do, instead of flying out in their own private superjetliner, railroad service in this country would soon be fit for human consumption again.

Same with getting to work. Every big shot big enough to make things happen arrives at the office in a chauffeured car, which then double parks at the door in case Mr. Shot decides on the spur of the moment, no time to look for distantly parked car, that he'll run out to California in his private superjetliner on which some poor oppressed woman dishwasher is scraping her knuckles off for an inefficient washing machine.

Then when people start throwing dishes the power crowd says, "Shame on you! What is a little thing like not finding a parking space, or not getting a good dishwash out of your machine, or taking the filthy, purposely uncomfortable train to California, compared to the great things you are doing under our inspired leadership to stop Communism cold?"

Stopping Communism is a great thing. In case the C.I.A. is tapping my brain, I want to get that thought clearly on record; but we would be better situated to admire it if we weren't too busy looking for parking space, trying to find a decent train to California, scraping the pots with sandpaper.

The trouble with America today is that people who have the power to make things happen don't live like other people do, so don't know what really needs to be made to happen. I just thought that a couple of minutes ago, you say? Oh well, I broke a cup a couple of minutes ago, too, but it didn't stop me from breaking another one just now.

What jackass poured cold gravy all over the floor?

....

NUMBERS IN WASHINGTON

Numbers in Washington are much easier to understand than in most places because there are only five. These are (1) the million, (2) the hundred million, (3) the billion, (4) the trillion and (5) the megaton.

In counting, strangers are often confused by the Washington system of modifying numbers with the phrases "give or take," "estimated at" and "on the order of magnitude of." Each of these phrases significantly alters the number's value.

For example, "twenty billion give or take a billion" means that the final cost of, say, a new submarine will probably not exceed the contractor's quoted price by more than three or four billion dollars.

By contrast, the expression "on the order of magnitude of

twenty billion dollars" means that the submarine will cost approximately thirty billion dollars, while "estimated at twenty billion dollars" means it will cost between forty and fifty billion dollars.

In general, "on the order of magnitude of" increases the value of the number by 50 percent, and "estimated at" increases it on the order of magnitude of 100 percent.

MARCH

IT IS GRAY and windy here and at night there is an evil white moon which laughs at the F.B.I.

MARCH

····· 10 ·····

From the birth of man until March 10, 1876, it was impossible for any man on earth to interrupt another man at dinner for the purpose of telling him, with the assistance of a machine and some wires, that he had been awarded a free dance lesson. Then—on this day just one hundred six years ago—at his home in Boston, Alexander Graham Bell placed the first telephone call. It went to Thomas Augustus Watson on another floor at Bell's house. Watson was not eating dinner. Bell did not attempt to sell him $399 worth of dance lessons. They did not even dawdle on the phone sighing and breathing; instead, Bell set a precedent for telephone use that has, regrettably, fallen into disuse. "Mr. Watson," he said, "come here; I want you."

Some years ago a man named Robert Townsend wrote a book in which he urged business executives to telephone themselves occasionally. "When you're off on a business trip or vacation, pretend you're a customer," he suggested. "Telephone some part of your organization and ask for help. You'll run into some real horror shows."

Mr. Townsend was offering a suggestion for checking up on how the company functioned when its face was turned to the world at large, instead of the boss. "Try calling yourself up," he proposed, "and see what indignities you've built into your own defenses."

This advice appeared in Mr. Townsend's book, *Up the Organization,* along with a great deal of other advice for successful corporate management. Because Mr. Townsend has successfully managed a corporation—Avis Rent A Car—it must be presumed that he knows his subject matter, but surely, in urging his readers to call themselves up, he is having his little joke.

A number of executives have tried over the years to catch themselves off guard by using the Townsend ruse, and it has invariably produced evil results. There was, to begin back in 1938, the incident of Gus Pappas, whose thriving hot-dog and chili parlor on South Carey Street in Baltimore was eventually, though years later, to bloom into a successful Italian restaurant.

While downtown one afternoon, Gus decided to test his telephone-answering procedures by telephoning his establishment and asking to speak to himself. His call was taken by Harry, his counter man. The instant Gus said, "I want to speak to Gus Pappas," Harry recognized Gus's voice.

Being a sensible man, Harry knew that no man in his right mind would spend a nickel—the price of a telephone call in those days—to speak to himself, and concluded that Gus must be having a mental collapse. Harry instantly saw that the problem was to get aid to Gus before he could harm himself.

Accordingly, Harry, whose naturally quick wit had been honed by Warner Brothers gangster movies, asked Gus to hold on. While Gus waited on the open line, Harry rushed next door to Bellinski's funeral parlor, telephoned the police, asked them to trace Gus's call and urged them to get to him immediately before something dreadful could happen.

Gus was in a drugstore telephone booth still hanging on when four Baltimore policemen seized him, placed him in restraints and removed him to the safety of the Central Police Station. Gus's explanation that he was telephoning himself for sound and sensible business reasons was eventually believed by the police doctors but that did not keep the story from spreading from Fremont Avenue to Monroe Street, an extensive area in which mothers cautioned their children, ineffectually of course, not to go near "that nut's hot dogs."

Gus eventually lived down his reputation and Harry went on to a long career in the C.I.A.

The outcome of Dick Orfling's attempt to reach himself by telephone was not so happy.

Until two years ago Dick was executive vice-president for General Consolidated's Rubber Heel Division with offices in Manhattan. Dick had reason to suspect that telephone answering in his office was being sloppily handled and, to test his suspicions, telephoned from Hannibal, Missouri, one day while on a road trip and asked to speak to Dick Orfling.

The call was immediately put through to his secretary. Speaking through a handkerchief, as he had seen spies do on television to disguise their voices, he said, "I'd like to speak to Mr. Orfling, please." "Who is calling?" she asked. "Ronald Jones," Dick said, using the pseudonym he had prepared. "Just a moment," his secretary said.

Almost immediately, a male voice came on the line. "Who is this?" asked Dick.

"Dick Orfling," the voice said.

"That's ridiculous," Dick said. "You can't possibly be Dick Orfling."

"I am much too busy to argue the point," the voice stated, and disconnected. Dick stifled the impulse to fly to New York immediately, although that night he did telephone home and found to his great relief that he was not there.

Next day Dick called from Butte and again asked to speak to himself. Upon being connected again, he asked himself how he was feeling. The voice that called its master Dick Orfling said, "Never better," and Dick said, "You won't remember me, but I'm Ronald Jones and we met—"

"Of course I remember you," said the voice. "You're that bogus name I sometimes use when I'm on the road and call myself up here at the office to see how the telephone is being answered."

Dick dropped the telephone and returned to New York on the next plane. Within six months his superiors were noting unhappily that Dick simply refused to travel and that, in consequence, the Rubber Heel Division was languishing. Dick is today a shell of the dynamic young executive of 1979 and has not answered the telephone in eighteen months without first insisting that his secretary find out if it is he who is calling. Usually he adds, "If it's me, tell me I'm not in."

....

PROBLEMS IN ETIQUETTE (1)

QUESTION: What should I do when no one will wait on me in restaurants? I recently took the girl I hoped to marry out to dinner, and after being seated, we sat at the table for an hour and ten minutes without anyone coming to take our order. My girl said I was the kind of person nobody paid any attention to, and now she has announced her engagement to marry another man, who can get waited on. How can I get waiters to pay attention to me?

ANSWER: After waiting twenty minutes without service, rise, go to the telephone, call one of the many establishments that deliver fried chicken or chop suey in large cardboard containers, and have them deliver your dinner to the table in the restaurant where the waiters refuse to wait on you. The arrival of your meal with its succulent aroma of chicken gravy or soy sauce, often borne by a man in white overalls, rarely fails to attract attention from the waiters, with whom you may then place an imperious order for coffee.

MARCH
······ 21 ······

Birth date of Johann Sebastian Bach in 1685

Someone did a study not long ago that deserves more attention than it has so far had. It showed that cows give less milk when they are milked in barns equipped with piped-in music.

This is mentioned here because it is vitally connected with the situation in our elevator at the office. There is an orchestra in our elevator. A group of us went aboard for a lift one morning and there it was, playing "Stardust" or maybe *Der Meistersinger von Nürnberg.* With this particular orchestra it is hard to tell because everything it plays sounds like everything else it plays.

It is the only orchestra in the world that can make

"Dardanella" sound exactly like "O Little Town of Bethlehem." It would be unpleasant enough having George Solti conducting the Chicago Symphony in the elevator, but an orchestra whose "Dark Town Strutter's Ball" sounds just like its "Battle Hymn of the Republic" is intolerable.

You start up on the elevator worrying about the Gross National Product, or wrestling with a tough narrative passage in the great American expense account which you are trying to compose, and this ridiculous orchestra begins pumping music out of the ceiling.

Yes, the ceiling. The orchestra sits in a little round box recessed in the elevator ceiling. Its conductor is Arturo Pastanini, a testy Neapolitan only three-eighths of an inch tall.

One funereal January morning while the elevator was filled with dreadful forebodings that winter would last another seven years, the orchestra struck up. It was maddening. That on a morning like that a man should have to listen to "O Little Town of Bethlehem"!

Although the elevator carried no other passengers, some protest seemed called for in the name of suffering humanity. "This is no time for 'O Little Town of Bethlehem,' you syrup pourers!" The orchestra played on.

"Shut up, up there!"

"If you don't like the music," shouted a tiny voice from the ceiling, "get out and walk!"

That was scary. The discreet move would have been to

get out and walk, but in the security of the office the insolence of the voice in the ceiling fed an anger that gradually conquered awe. Back to the elevator. Down it started, "O Little Town of Bethlehem" oozing from the ceiling.

"Call yourselves musicians, up there? If you're musicians, why can't you play anything except 'O Little Town of Bethlehem'?" No reply. At the bottom, the elevator took on passengers. We all ascended quietly while the orchestra played on.

After the passengers had debarked the elevator started down. "What right does an orchestra have to take over an elevator and entertain me against my will, eh? Answer me that, up there!"

"Basta!" screamed the tiny voice. The screen covering the recessed hole in the ceiling slid back a fraction of an inch. An angry face peered down. It was the little maestro himself, Signor Pastanini. "Listen, swindler," he said, "why don't you get back to falsifying your expense account and leave honest musicians to make an honest living in peace?"

"Ha! You call it an honest living drooling that fifteenth-rate music over everybody who has to use an elevator? If I wanted a concert in the elevator, I'd wear a tuxedo to the office."

Halfway through this conversation the elevator had stopped and taken on two passengers. There was a ghastly silence while they rode down and debarked, and as the elevator ascended again Pastanini indulged himself in a dirty laugh. "By tea time," he said, "it will be all over the building that you are talking to yourself in the elevator." And he closed the recess cover its fraction of an inch and disappeared.

He was right. By late afternoon, the office boys were full of hooded smiles. Next morning the boss suggested that a short vacation might be in order. It seemed wise to behave more cautiously in the elevator for a while, but one Saturday when the building was almost deserted curiosity asserted itself.

"Pastanini!" (A mere whisper.) "Pastanini! You're really up there, aren't you?"

The music dripped down in glutinous globules. "Why did they put you up there, Maestro?" A tiny teardrop fell.

"Once," he said, "I played to a cow from a hole in the ceiling of a milking barn, my object being to increase her milk production. Instead, my music drove down milk production. I was about to be fired when someone had a brilliant idea. 'If we put him in an office-building elevator,' they said, 'maybe he will drive down expense-account production.' "

MORAL: If you can't fool the cows, try the sheep.

MARCH

⋯ 24 ⋯

You will have noticed by this time that there are noises in the earth. Something is going on.

The first warm day occurred and everybody went out of doors singing, "Hurray, hurray for the first warm day" and, "The robin is icumen in."

"What is the happy occasion?" asked a misanthrope. "Has science conquered the common cold?"

"It's spring! It's spring! And the bird is on the wing."

"Humbug!" said the mean man. "What is the winging bird to you?"

"I have survived another winter."

"Nonsense," said the misanthrope. "You are simply another year older. What has survived another winter is the crab grass and the poison ivy while you, having aged another year, are slowly losing the strength to fight them."

"But April is coming, man! Can't you taste it on the wind?"

"April is the cruelest month, breeding tax bills out of the dead bank balance," the misanthrope said.

"Ah, but the world is greening and the bud is pink on the rose cane."

"And what does it mean to you?" sneered the misanthrope. "As the sap rises the bagworm will resume eating your cypress, and the thrips, the leaf mold, the brown spot and the bole canker will rot out your rose canes. Your cypress is mangy enough already. The bagworm should finish it this spring. Return to your fireside and pray for the return of the glaciers to save you from the thrips, the mold, the canker and the bagworm, as well as the crab grass and the poison ivy."

"What! And miss the blooming of the girls? Soon now they will ungirt their girdles and go through the streets intoxicating mankind with memory and desire."

"Girt or ungirt, they are all the same," said the misanthrope. "To the single man they will bring expense and discontent, and to the married man they will bring discontent and expense. They exploit the male's spring foolishness by ungirding and inducing discontent and ridiculous expenditure. Retire to your den and do not come out until summer, when the heated humidity will not only have dampened your ardor but will also have shown you that it is foolish to expect anything of spring but a summer that makes you yearn for winter."

"But spring is the season of hope, and without hope what would man be?"

"He would be less foolish. Listen to me and believe me when I tell you that there is not a chance in the world that the New York Mets will win the pennant, that you will receive a vice-presidency, that your children will win scholarships to Harvard and Stanford, or that your car will get through the summer without at least one $165.95 repair bill."

"Ah, my friend, in any other season I would dismiss you as a carrier of the messages of death, but not in spring. Spring creates these strange sweet moods and makes me do things of inexplicable tenderness."

"Yes," said the misanthrope, "I notice that you are standing out here watering the sidewalk with your garden hose. I assume that you are not watering your garden because it is already too wet with spring mud, but that, feeling the urge to water something simply because it is spring, you are lavishing gallons of precious water on concrete."

"Spring makes me want to do something for the sidewalk. I cannot explain it, good misanthrope."

"Take my advice," said the misanthrope. "Go into your cellar and start storing this precious water in radiation-proof containers. If there is no bombing, there will certainly be a drought, and if there is neither, the world will certainly come to an end one way or the other. With plenty of stored water, you can last a long time down there in the cellar."

"Spring is too wonderful to be spent in a cellar storing water for the end of the world."

The misanthrope strode away smiling contentedly about the asininity of mankind. "Spring madness," he muttered. "Wait until the end of the world comes. Then you'll be sorry."

A small March cloud sailed up, parked overhead and cheerfully blew his hat off.

···········

INVENTOR OF PRAGMATISM

The inventor of Pragmatism was Giovanni Pragma, an eccentric nineteenth-century Florentine, who, after a series of comic misadventures, was elected to the Florence city council as a sort of municipal joke.

Enunciating the principle that the test of action should be not, "Is it philosophically sound?" but, "Will it work?" Pragma was abandoned by his wife early in his career after insisting that they try maintaining separate households to see if it would work.

"It is philosophically unsound," Signora Pragma said, upon leaving him.

"But how do you know it won't work?" Pragma retorted.

Later Pragma was badly crippled while trying to fly off Giotto's bell tower in a large pair of eagle wings. "It won't work," he said upon recovery. Elected to the city council, he amused Italy for years with his plan to fling two dozen new bridges across the Arno and build an eight-lane cartway from Florence to Rome.

"It will work," he insisted. "It will solve the traffic problem."

"It will work, all right," the mayor agreed, "but it is philosophically unsound to ruin the city and countryside in order to make it easier for more people to crowd into the Uffizi Gallery when we ourselves can already hardly see the Raphaels because of the crowding."

Pragmatism died of laughter in Italy but survived by leaping the Atlantic. This is why Florentines say, "America is a nice place to visit, but you'd need an aqualung to live there."

....

The dirty work at political conventions is almost always done in the grim hours between midnight and dawn. Hangmen and politicians work best when the human spirit is at its lowest ebb.

APRIL

*APRIL DIVERTS our attention from life's inevitabili-
ties and focuses it on the potentialities. In April, if the
glands still work properly, it is possible to see the world
as it might be if only it were not the world.*

APRIL

..... 2 .....

This is the time when all cares are set aside while America wonders: Who will win the Academy Awards this year? Who will be unfairly denied once again the Oscar he/she has so long deserved? Who will weep wet joy clasping statuette to bosom while thanking Mother, Beethoven, Homer, Francis X. Bushman, Good Queen Bess, Cervantes, Frances Parkinson Keyes, the Eastman Kodak Company and the U. S. Marines for making possible this chance to weep? O tempora, O Hollywood, O Movies Around the World! What would life be without them!

For those of us who saw the British Empire built on Saturday afternoons in the 1930s while we sat in the dark chewing Mary Jane bars and kneading Jujubes between sweaty palms, one of the saddest events of the modern age was England's abandonment of the cinematic world east of Suez. A succession of dim Prime Ministers in unpressed suits did the deed—forgettable men with almost forgotten names. Harold Macmillan. Harold Wilson. It was a time of Harolds quietly reducing England to minipower, a time that made us aging movie fans despair at the speed with which our favorite empire could be ground to dust.

Was it for this, we wondered, that Franchot Tone endured the tyranny of Captain Bligh and survived to sweep the seas for England? C. Aubrey Smith, surely, would never have permitted it. "You Harolds," he would have said, "turn in your epaulets and batmen and consider yourselves under house arrest. The rest of the regiment marches at dawn to relieve Gordon at Khartoum."

C. Aubrey Smith, alas, is gone with the Empire, and the only man left standing between England and total minipower is Mick Jagger. Good as he is, Jagger can never inspire us with the confidence we felt in Ronald Colman, the conqueror of India, or in Tyrone Power, the founder of Lloyd's of London.

Many of us still have a large emotional investment in the Empire we saw built in those Saturday matinees. They made us all imperialists in the same vague sense that the Westerns made us all racists. Who, after all, could possibly cheer for Eduardo Ciannelli's pit of cobras when Gunga Din—"You're a better man than I am, Sam Jaffe" —was willing to die to save India for the Queen, God save her?

The standard British Empire film, in fact, was little

more than the Western in a South Kensington accent. Even Gary Cooper at one point changed from chaps to jodhpurs long enough to head 'em off at Khyber Pass. Instead of turkey feathers, the bad guys usually wore turbans. The regiment marched to bagpipes instead of bugles, but this did not prevent it from arriving invariably in the nick of time.

It is fashionable now to feel guilty about having once enjoyed this type of entertainment. What those cowboys were really engaged in, enlightened modern thought has it, was genocide. What C. Aubrey Smith and the thin red line were up to, obviously, was the propagation of colonialism, a very bad thing for a person to confess nowadays to having once cheered for.

Such reasoning is nonsense. The fact of the matter is that at the time the British Empire romances were most popular in the United States, the modern Englishman was held in such universal scorn in this country that, when dealt with at all in films, he was never depicted as anything but a silly ass.

The Empire is gone, leaving us only with a few scratches on our minds. No longer will we sit past midnight to watch Errol Flynn lead the charge of the light brigade into the valley of aspirin and deodorant commercials without thinking, "All, all for naught."

Echoing down distant corridors of the mind from time to time we will catch snatches of far-away conversation. "The telegraph lines are cut between Rawalpindi and Omdurman, colonel."

"You know what this means, of course."

"Abner Biberman has seized Lahore and is marching on Nairobi with two hundred thousand crazed fanatics."

"Only one man south of the Hindu Kush can save India for the Queen."

"You mean—?"

"Douglas Fairbanks, Jr."

And we will be torn between the urge to cry, "Head Biberman off at the Khyber Pass, Doug, Jr.," and the impulse to moan, "Don't send that boy up in that old crate held together with nothing but chewing gum and baling wire, C. Aubrey. There's no saving the Empire. It's doomed to the trivia of the twentieth century."

"What! See England knuckle to this strutting popinjay from Corsica, man!" (How easy it is still to hear C. Aubrey.) "Turn in your Mary Jane bars and Jujubes and go below, Mr. Christian. Nelson bids farewell to Vivien Leigh in Culver City at dawn and sails with the fleet for Trafalgar."

It was all a mockery, C. Aubrey. Pull back the regiment before the Mahdi attacks. Recall Robert Taylor to Waterloo Bridge. Tell Tyrone Power he's wasting his time digging the Suez Canal. It will all end in Wimpy burgers.

"As God is my witness, sir, Whitehall shall hear of this. Clear the poop deck and report to the regimental mess at dawn to relieve the garrison at Bhowani Junction. England expects that every Jujube chewer will do his duty. We sail on the first tide to meet the Spanish Armanda for good Queen Bette Davis."

It's useless, C. Aubrey. In the end there will be nothing but the Harolds and Mick Jagger.

"Nonsense, lad. If the Harolds last a thousand years, men will still say, 'Let's catch their finest hour on The Late Show.'"

....

The magic of children is their ability to cloud our memories so that when we look back we recall only the golden moments, the sweet laughter and the sentimental tears, and none of the awful trials. What we forget is that parenthood is also going through with the P.T.A. again, being humiliated by a fourteen-year-old at Indian wrestling, having a daughter in love with a saxophone player, snarling about book reports for fifteen years, going mad in the multiplication tables and trying to persuade a nine-year-old that he must learn about Leonid Brezhnev or be turned down by Harvard.

APRIL

..... **8** .....

Some things simply cannot be overlooked. This almanac does not concede the existence of Adolf Hitler's birthday, celebrate the invention of political

propaganda or note the identity of the man whose idea it was to market frozen French-fried potatoes. A few concessions to uglier realities must be made, however. You have exactly one week longer to file your Federal Income Tax return. Spend this week wisely.

CORRESPONDENCE FILE

Collector of Internal Revenue
Washington, D.C.

Sir:

My friend Hauser tells me that he is going to pay less in taxes than I this year because he has bought a building that is depreciating. I understand that if one has invested in something that is depreciating the Government will allow him to deduct enough from his usual tax bill to vacation in Jamaica. Unfortunately, I am unable to find the correct table for calculating my own windfall under this provision. I am forty-nine years old and have been depreciating at a terrifying rate for the past fifteen years. I have invested large sums of capital, energy, faith and time in myself, and would now like to vacation in Jamaica. Will you please send me the appropriate form for computing my depreciation allowance?

Yours truly,
Botford Gill

Dear Mr. Gill:

If you are a building, the Government is just as concerned about you as it is about Mr. Hauser's building and is perfectly willing, in order to promote the nation's economic growth, to allow the persons speculating in you the financial wherewithal to vacation in Jamaica. The schedule for depreciating buildings is enclosed.

Sincerely,
Collector of Internal Revenue

Dear Collector:

Do I write like a building?

Yours truly,
Botford Gill

Dear Mr. Gill:

You write like a man who has been so improvident that he has failed to build himself any tax shelters in the past year and is now so angry that he doesn't want to see Mr. Hauser have a good time in Jamaica. If, however, you are a building, will you please forward to your owners the depreciation schedules enclosed in my last letter so that they may plan their vacations?

Sincerely,

Dear Collector:

Since I last wrote, I have run into my friends Carlin and Herpel. Carlin says that as a result of his buying oil wells, you are giving him back enough of his tax money to vacation in Switzerland, and Herpel says that as a result of his buying municipal bonds he is getting back enough to buy a small republic in Central America.

If I had known when I was young that you would not give me back any of my tax money at all as a result of my buying food, clothing and a TV set, I would have gone into oil-well buying or municipal-bond purchases years ago and might now be able to afford a little vacation in Jamaica.

I assume, since you don't earn any money yourself, that you are using my tax payments to send those remittances to Hauser, Carlin and Herpel. As I see it, this makes Hauser, Carlin and Herpel my dependents. May I claim them as dependents and take three additional exemptions on my income tax? This would not get me to Jamaica, but it might finance a motel weekend at the Luray Caverns.

Yours truly,

Dear Mr. Gill:
No.

Yours sincerely,

Dear Collector:
How about this? Hauser, Carlin and Herpel have a large investment in me, as will be seen if you consider the workings of your tax system. Among the three of them they contribute just enough taxes to the Government to prevent my taxes from rising to such a level that I would

be unable to buy food. Thus, their combined tax payments amount to an investment in keeping me alive so that I can remain available to pay you the money that you require to provide them with Central American republics and Jamaica vacations.

In my view, they should be entitled to depreciate me, as I am obviously not going to be able to produce my present level of tax payments for their benefit much longer at my present rate of depreciation. Between us, I calculate that Hauser and Carlin might be willing to give me 10 per cent of any additional tax savings they earn from depreciating me. (Herpel would plow it all back into tax-free municipals.) I figure this might be enough to finance a January week in Atlantic City with my wife, though of course I'd pay the usual tax on the sums I received from Hauser and Carlin in token of my depreciation.

Will you kindly send me some appropriate forms for my friends?

Yours sincerely,

So far there has been no reply to this letter. The Internal Revenue people are not interested in irony, especially when it begins to increase their postage bill.

....

The trouble with a government that travels by limousine is that it is out of touch with the world it is supposed to serve. Put a man in a limousine and you loosen his grasp on life's realities.

He sees a world where all traffic policemen are good fellows, all doormen are saints and all women are sweet-tempered. In the limousine world there is no such thing as a speed limit, an illegal left turn or a forbidden parking space. To the limousined man, a traffic jam is merely an opportunity to work on his briefcase in peace, and a storm only a spectacle to be enjoyed from the bathyscaphic security of custom-made cushions. No wonder such people are so often heard complaining about the public's poor grasp of the world's harsh realities.

APRIL

······ 16 ······

On this day, soured by yesterday's experience with the tax collector, soothe your spirits by acting as the government does. Look around the house for deadbeats who have not paid you what they owe and, if they refuse to come across, put their feet to the fire.

Sometimes bad ideas get themselves sanctified. This happened some years ago in a movie called *Fahrenheit 451,* which set out to show us one of those depressing visions of a future world stewing in its own futuristic evil. And how do we know it is evil? Because it burns books.

Its hero, a "fireman," spends his working hours—at least until he becomes confused—clanging about town putting books to the torch. "Oh," we are urged to emote, "what a terrible, terrible world it is that will put book burners on the city payroll!" If we start thinking about the idea, however, the whole movie collapses.

Anyone who acquires books immediately senses that the premise of the film is false. Instead of being horrified, he asks, "What's wrong with having a fire department ready to rush out to the house day or night to burn a stack of books?" In fact, the script writer had a good idea and abandoned it for another mindless sermon against book burning.

This notion that book burning is bad seems to have become embedded in the American mind during the time of Adolf Hitler, who practiced it in the foolish delusion that an idea can be killed by burning the paper on which it is jotted down.

Americans have alway known better. We have always known that the surest way to get a book read by people who never read anything is to get it banned in Boston. But in our antipathy to Nazism, we subscribed to the belief that ideas can indeed be sent up in smoke. And so today it is still almost impossible for an American to make a bonfire of books.

With this taboo working for their preservation, books have acquired a sacred quality that is shared by no other medium of expression. Let us say that a general has a few forgettable ideas about NATO. If we see him expounding them on television, we may listen and forget.

If the general expresses his ideas in a newspaper, we feel no hesitation about throwing the newspaper out in the next day's trash. If in a magazine, we feel no twinges of incipient Nazism by using the magazine to light a fire.

But let him spin out his idea to sixty thousand words, have them packaged between two pieces of pasteboard and placed on the coffee table, and the general becomes part of your household for life. When the family moves, he moves with it, along with the dog and the goldfish. He has to be dusted year in, year out. He sits there on the shelf, while the children grow, marry and drift out of your life; when you die, lawyers have to be paid to decide who must support him for the next sixty years.

These days when the publishing industry grinds out books like sausages, household living space shrinks rapidly as the general moves in along with his cronies—the diplomat worried about the Liberian balance of payments, the lawyer who once sued Howard Hughes, the fellow who spent two weeks among Afghan tribesmen, the woman who wanted you to know what it was like to be a Jewish housewife in Madison, Wisconsin.

Some forty thousand new books are published every year in this country. Most of them your friends won't even borrow, and if they do they never forget to return them. You can give them away to servicemen, if you have no conscience at all, or to the parish book sale, or the Salvation Army, but that begs the issue. It simply means somebody else must support them.

Putting them in the trash is almost as grave a social offense as burning them. And yet, at the rate they are being produced something must be done with them if they are not to end up occupying most of the house space in America.

The rational solution is foreseen, and then witlessly attacked, in *Fahrenheit 451.* Book burning will have to be made an honorable trade, like garbage disposal. When it is, we shall be able once a year to lay an avenging hand upon the authors who have been lying around the house for a generation.

"Sorry, fellows," we shall be able to say at last, "but you have been mooching off me for twenty-five years without earning your keep."

"The firemen are on their way!" we shall shout to our wives.

"Throw down all books whose titles contain the words 'Strategy,' 'Crisis,' 'Atlantic,' 'Society,' 'Power,' 'The West,' 'The Day,' 'How to,' 'De Gaulle,' 'Tito,' 'Danger,' 'Freedom,' 'World,' 'Survival' and 'Creative.' "

And while our wives heap high the pile, the rest of us will scan jacket blurbs and start throwing on every book described as "wise and witty," "sensitive and perceptive," "haunting," "shocking," "tender and insightful," "searing," "challenging," "brilliantly funny," "hilarious and fascinating," "particularly lucid," "charged with suspense and narrative drive," "terrifyingly detailed," "stark" and "bold, brilliant and revealingly candid."

If publishers conceive their function to be the reduction of literature to hamburger, we should feel no guilt about barbecuing it.

APRIL
...... 24 ......

This is one of the most historic days in the history of the automobile and, therefore, of America. On this day in 1908, Mr. and Mrs. Jacob Murdock and their three children left—where else?—Los Angeles in a Packard, bound for New York. They made it—32 days, 5 hours and 25 minutes after departure—and so became the first American family to cross the country by car in fast enough time to make others want to try it. Thus was born the Interstate Highway System.

The dramatic difference between Los Angeles and other cities is that in Los Angeles everybody lives in automobiles. Distances are so great and mass transportation so poor that there are no alternatives. As a result, the people of Los Angeles have become so accustomed to driving everywhere that most of them have forgotten there is any other way to live. It is routine for them to drive next door to borrow a cup of flour. Sleepwalking is unknown. It has been replaced by sleepdriving.

Walking, in any condition, is regarded as prima facie evidence of felonious intent. In Beverly Hills, anyone who commits walking after dusk is liable to police interrogation. The offense is known as "pedestrianism," though more enlightened legalists argue that it should be viewed by society as a sickness, like kleptomania, rather than as a criminal offense.

The social base of the automotive way of life is the splendid system of turnpikes, called "freeways," which bind the sprawling vastness into a single city. The person visiting Los Angeles for the first time approaches the freeways with the terror of the infantryman about to taste his first combat, since the traffic may be moving bumper-to-bumper at seventy miles an hour. The person who successfully manages to maneuver into it from an access ramp without losing more than two fenders is said to have been "blooded."

Once accustomed to the pace, the visitor feels some of the exhilaration that the natives derive from freeway driving as he roars past jack-knifed tractors and twenty-car pile-ups and nimbly avoids the steel piping and two-by-fours that bounce off speeding trucks in their zeal to cut a Volkswagen out of the middle lane.

Most of the vital life processes can be, and are, experienced on the freeway. Take the fairly typical case of Gladwin Gordon, a San Pedro front-end aligner, who is as much at home on a freeway as an aspirin is on a television tube.

G.G., as his friends call him, met his wife, Eliza, when their cars were stalled side by side for six hours one Sunday afternoon on the Santa Ana Freeway. G.G. was on his way to align a front end in Orange County, and Eliza was headed for a drive-in mortuary to pay her last respects to a dead uncle.

By the time the traffic jam began to move their acquaintance had deepened into something profound, and by the time traffic had resumed its seventy-mile-an-hour pace, G.G. was shouting his proposal of marriage from his Pontiac to her Mercedes. Eliza accepted at the Harbor Boulevard exit in Anaheim.

They were married at a drive-in chapel and honeymooned on the freeway to Santa Monica. Unfortunately, the marriage came to a bad end when they had to stop for gasoline. At that point both made the mistake of leaving their cars. Eliza saw that G.G. was only 4 feet 11 inches tall, and G.G. saw that Eliza was 6 feet 4 and weighed 225 pounds.

They were divorced on the Harbor Freeway in Inglewood, but it was too late to prevent delivery three days later of a tiny little sports car, ordered by G.G. on his car telephone when the ecstasy of their union was at its height. The court awarded custody of the sports car to the Mercedes.

G.G., in order to meet his support payments, had to sell his Pontiac. Utterly unwheeled, he began to go to pieces and took to walking late at night when he thought no one would catch him. Soon his entire block was terrorized with rumors that a phantom pedestrian was on the loose, but G.G. became so cunning about hiding in palm-tree shadows that police dragnets were unable to find him. That block might be terrorized to this day by pedestrianism had G.G. not suffered a post-pedestrian seizure of remorse one night and written the police an anonymous note pleading, "Please catch me before I walk again!"

To mail it, of course, he had to walk to the mailbox, which he thoughtlessly did in broad daylight next morning. He was only halfway there when he was surrounded, captured and nearly lynched by a terrified mob of automobiles.

Returned to society after two years of psychotherapy, G.G. is now rehabilitated, back on the freeway and happily married to a woman he met in a used Buick that he was about to overtake near the Civic Center. It has been a good marriage. G.G. hasn't had the urge to take a walk in nearly two years, and he and his wife never stop for gasoline at the same filling station.

INSIDE FACTS ABOUT PROGRESS (1)

Progress is what people who are planning to do something really terrible almost always justify themselves on the grounds of.

MAY

WHO AMONG US has not changed his mind about sitting on his front lawn some balmy spring night because he has suddenly realized that passing motorists might stone him to death with empty beer cans?

MAY

⋯⋯ 15 ⋯⋯

If you have an unheated attic, it should be warm enough now to get up there and do the spring house-cleaning. Be ruthless about throwing away worn-out articles for which there can be no possible future use, or they will start piling up around the house, even in the living room.

"Just for a few minutes," Robert's wife whispered. "He is very weak."

He did not look unusually weak, slouched in his favorite armchair in the corner, the room smelling of petty failure. "It's good to see you, Robert, but they tell me I can only stay a few minutes."

"What a marvelously wooden, time-consuming, roundabout, old-fashioned greeting," said Robert. "That's one thing I always liked about you. Your wonderful reluctance to commit yourself immediately on entering rooms. Very quaint, but terribly hypocritical these days. I don't imagine you're going to last long either."

"You're looking fine, Robert. Just fine."

"Don't talk that archaic old nonsense," Robert said. "You've heard the news. It's all over."

"Oh, just because you're a slight bit irrelevant—"

"A slight bit! That's good. A slight bit irrelevant! Last month, which was the last time I set foot out of this room, I wasn't being relevant more than ten minutes a day."

"They can do something these days about that sort of thing, Robert. Johns Hopkins. Massachusetts General. Great advances are being made. Have you thought of a relevance transplant?"

Robert waved impatiently. "You really think a relevance transplant would help, don't you? If I could be relevant four hours a day, you think, I'd be as good as new. Isn't that it?"

"Many persons with only four hours of daily relevance capacity hold very respectable positions nowadays, Robert."

Robert's laugh was bitter. "Suppose I could be relevant twenty hours a week," he said. "What good would it do? I can't work up any rage or fury. I can't even hate hypocrisy anymore. Between us, in fact, there is a great deal of hypocrisy that I find rather charming."

"I am certain you don't mean that, Robert. Not in your heart of hearts. Those are the anguished words of a man in terminal irrelevance and, as such, may be forgiven you."

"Come here," Robert beckoned. "Come a little closer. I want to whisper something."

"I don't want to hear any of your blasphemy against commitment, Robert. No matter what you say, you've always been a man of commitment with a decent hatred for hypocrisy."

Robert grinned. "I don't believe in relevance," he whispered.

"Those are terrible words to speak at the end, Robert."

He sobbed a good bit then, and when he regained self-control he said, "The truth is, I never believed in relevance. Relevance was against everything I had devoted my life to."

"And what was that, Robert?"

"To solving the leisure-time problem," he said.

Well, you may imagine what a shock it was to hear, in that strange room, someone mention the leisure-time problem again. The leisure-time problem had been the big problem of 1962, and like all the big-problems-of-the-year since then—from physical fitness to air pollution —it had been put aside unsolved so that we could get on to new big problems that we wouldn't have time to solve.

Robert, however, had never abandoned the leisure-time problem and in fact had come quite close to solving it, when his experiments were confounded by the emergence of the irrelevance problem.

The difficulty, you see, rose from Robert's conclusion that the most fruitful thing to do with leisure in ninety-seven cases out of a hundred, was something that was almost utterly irrelevant, such as the mastery of integral calculus, making oil copies of the old masters, bicycling, and so forth.

Imagine the plight of a man happily copying the old masters and bicycling, suddenly attacked by enraged haters of irrelevance and noncommitment, who were too young ever to have heard of the leisure-time problem.

For a moment there it was almost possible to sympathize with Robert. But no man of integrity can ignore the social evil caused by irrelevance in high places. At least for the next few months.

....

How many more years will our educators continue to lecture us on the evils of whipping the children until they bring home high grades? Year after year we listen to these fellows tell us that it is not the grade that counts, but the development of the child's personality. After the lecture they go back to all the best schools and reject our children because they have C averages.

MAY

····· 22 ·····

What sweeter words can fall on the human ear? It's going to be May all week long!

It is a beautiful May morning. Sunlight streams through the window. Birds chatter, the heady odor of wisteria floats on the exhaust fumes. Suddenly, for no logical reason at all, you feel good.

Alarms sound throughout the city, warning the populace that someone has awakened feeling good and will soon be moving through its streets, corridors, fluorescent cells. A smiler is within the gates. Orders are dispatched along the extrasensory communications net that binds the city's defense system.

"Report of a man feeling good at Elm and Main. Use extreme caution! May be happy!"

It is a terrible situation, but exhilarating for all that. Soon the whole city will be after you. Is it best to give up immediately? That would be the easy way normally, but there is no getting around the fact that you feel good, really good, and if you are cunning and brave maybe you can take a few down smiling with you before you are zapped.

"Feeling good, aren't you?" says rather than asks the woman making breakfast. She is hooked into the warning net, too.

"Can you ever forgive me, Emma? I didn't mean to feel good. I just woke up this morning and the sunlight was streaming in and there was the smell of wisteria on the exhaust fumes . . ."

"You have no right to feel good. Don't you realize you can't just wake up feeling good whenever there's a little sunlight? If you'd think about my miseries once in a while instead of your own selfish pleasures, you wouldn't be in this predicament."

As she natters on you realize that she is stalling for time until the psychiatrist can get there. Over the back fence you go and down the alley, smiling at dogs.

At the bus stop a familiar face (Tom's) registers surprise and hostility. "You've got your nerve!"

"I can't help myself, Tom."

"How can you feel good when you think about all the poor people there are?"

"The sunlight was so lovely . . ."

"You're a disgrace to your class."

"I hate myself for not being poor, Tom, but I just can't stop feeling good in spite of it."

At the office it is even worse. A picket line of idealists is tearing up the cobblestones. "Are you the man who feels good?" their leader demands.

"Me? You must be insane. How could anyone even think of feeling good when he contemplates his own personal responsibility for social injustice, oppression of women, the lack of love in the world, Christopher Columbus, the Crusades, old Pharaoh, Kaiser Wilhelm, Mussolini, and the population explosion?"

It is a close thing, but the chief idealist buys it. "Okay," he grunts. "Have a dyspeptic day."

It makes you feel really good to put one over on an idealist. In fact, it makes you feel so good that you feel bad about it. What are you, anyhow? Some kind of a social fink? Everyone else can wake up with the sunshine streaming through the window without letting it make him feel good.

In the office Miss Pansky is near tears. "You! Of all people!" she cries. "Just last night I was telling my roommate what a beautiful sense of guilt you had."

"I didn't mean to feel good, Miss Pansky. The sunlight—"

" 'He'll never let himself quit despairing for a minute,' I told my roommate. 'Not as long as there are nuclear weapons and unsafe autos and bad boys and teams that lose at football.' "

"Would it help if I told you honestly that feeling good makes me feel like an absolute rat?"

"Don't go for your smile!"

It is the misery squad. The jig is up. They carry tear gas.

Now you must be reclaimed for society. The psychiatrist is so understanding. "When you thought you were feeling good this morning, what was it you were really feeling?" And so on. In no time at all he proves that it is utterly impossible for you ever to have felt good at any time in your life or ever to feel good at any time in the future.

How sweet is the absolution! How understanding is the entire society that you have nearly destroyed! You have learned your lesson. Misery no longer loves company. Nowadays it insists upon it.

MISERY, SECURITY AND HAPPINESS (3)

Misery is going to New York on your honeymoon and finding that the hotel has put you in a room on an airshaft.

Security is a smile from a headwaiter.

Happiness is when a wire has become disconnected under the dashboard and the motor is hissing and you go to a garage and the repairman says you have a "vacuum leak" and you ask him how much it will cost to repair and he says, "$1.75."

MAY

⋯⋯ 31 ⋯⋯

The Reverend Doctor Norman Vincent Peale, the father of positive thinking, was born this day in 1898 in Bowersville, Ohio.

Bill and Cora Sue Gorth are different from most young couples nowadays. For one thing, they talk just the way people in television commercials talk. You know, no pronouns in front of their verbs and lots of imbecilic gushing about scouring powder and cuticle softener.

"Fabulous!" Cora Sue is always saying, followed by something like, "Scours twice as clean as my old sink scourer," or "Softens cuticle twice as fast as my old softening product," and so on. At first it makes your flesh crawl to hear them.

They are not to be laughed away, however, for in an age when man's natural unhappiness is heightened by loss of religious faith, the Gorths have found happiness through faith in television. "Absolute faith in the doctrine of materialism as revealed on Channels 2, 4, 5, 7, 9 and 20," says Bill, "has made a new person of me."

"Fabulous," says Cora Sue. "Twice as much happiness power as my old faith product."

Bill's conversion began one day when, listless, Vietnam-weary and tired of his marriage, he sat in the evening traffic jam, slouched at the wheel of his Hupmobile. "Suddenly," he says, "I realized that it wasn't happening. When I got home that night I told Cora Sue, 'We've got to find something that will make it happen.' That night Channel 4 spoke to me for the first time. 'Rhinoceros makes it happen,' Channel 4 said."

Bill immediately bought a sporty new Rhinoceros with the sleek roach-tail trunk line and synchro-glandular transmission on the tape deck, and that very afternoon it happened. Ten women threw themselves at his roach-tail trunk, his wife fell in love with him again, the afternoon traffic jam dissolved and Bill's biceps became five inches larger.

"Fabulous," Cora Sue recalls. "Twice as much cigarette consumption as my old marriage product, too."

Seeing Bill's new happiness, Cora Sue began taking

instruction from Channel 9. One night after Bill had hitched his Rhinoceros at the curb and fought off the beauties swarming to kiss him, he entered the kitchen to find Cora Sue wearing a queen's crown. That afternoon, on instruction from Channel 9, she had quit greasing the bread with the high-priced spread and had switched to new improved Gummoid Margarine.

Since that day, both Gorths have become contented, if somewhat hysterical, people. This gives an odd quality to attempts to make conversation with them. Commonplace conversational gambits such as, "Why am I so miserable all the time?" bring answers such as, "It's that old product you're using on your hair, friend. Can't stand the wind-tunnel test. Leaves a thick, ugly coat of grease on your forehead. Try new improved scalp mucilage. Keeps hair neat all day long. Makes girls purr."

"Fabulous," says Cora Sue. "Twice as much anti-misery power, too."

Like so many converts, the Gorths have no patience with skeptics. "What! Not believe in the new washday miracle?" Bill will ask. "Why, man, you might as well deny the existence of twice as much anti-perspirant power. You might as well say there is no crunchy goodness flavor-packed into every wholesome kernel of springtime freshness."

Nothing irritates Bill Gorth more than someone's pointing out that he talks like a fool. "Of course I talk like a fool," he says. "Cora Sue and I both talk like fools. It is our way of being absolutely faithful to our beliefs.

Look, this whole neighborhood, this whole city, this whole country is swarming with people who practice the same faith we do. The only difference is that they're ashamed of it. It conceals their shame if they can laugh at the language of the channels, but it doesn't stop them from living by the message. Cora Sue and I believe in being perfectly honest about our faith."

"Fabulous," says Cora Sue. "Twice as much fool-exposure power, too."

Happiness to Bill and Cora Sue is belief in faster starting, brighter laundry, quicker relief, fresher smoke, longer protection, shinier floors, crunchier goodness, crispier chips, sexier lips, slimmer hips and happier trips.

"As a religion," says Bill, "I'll admit it's not much, but at least it is suited to today's civilization."

"Fabulous," says Cora Sue. "Twice as much fun as that old morality, too."

....

The people who are always hankering loudest for some golden yesteryear usually drive new cars.

....

One of the most dangerous areas in the world is the notorious Horse's Mouth. It is an undulating swampy area bounded on the north by the White House and on the south by the Pentagon and is densely infested with people who are certain they know what is going on in El Salvador.

JUNE

JUNE HITS TOWN one midnight and a few days later she's got those lightning bugs going. Then she brings up that big stupid moon of hers and starts dangling wild roses, and before you know it, people are getting married in droves.

JUNE

····· 1 ·····

June is famous for marriage and, at its start, we shall
all be better for a few moments of reflection upon the
sea of matrimony and the adventures awaiting all
those who sail it.

In a hair-raising article some time back entitled "How
Women Really Get Husbands," *Cosmopolitan* magazine
told the story of a spineless fellow named Allen who
found himself trapped between a cynical divorcee and a
hysterical mother. It went like this:

On discovering that Allen has been courting the divorced woman, whose name is Dorothy, Mother threatens suicide, whereupon Allen joins the Army to escape
Dorothy's tears and Mother's threats of self-destruction.
We need no more facts to see at this stage that Dorothy
is a lucky girl. Dorothy, however, is not as smart as we
are.

Does she shout a thankful "Good riddance!" and go looking for a more normal man to mate with? She does not. Women in *Cosmopolitan* never do. In *Cosmopolitan*'s view of the sexes, "the mating market place" is rife with "jungle warfare." ("When love doesn't come flying at you out of the blue, you find yourself pursuing it.")

And so, Dorothy sets a trap for Allen. To win Allen's mother, she writes "a real tear-jerker" of a letter— "more sobs per line than Louisa May Alcott . . . what a wonderful son Mamma raised . . . she'd only try to be as good a wife as Mamma was," and so forth.

Poor Allen. "Mamma burst into tears. 'I was wrong,' she told Allen, 'You've got to marry that girl.'" Having lost his only out, Allen had no choice.

What *Cosmopolitan* does not point out is that while Allen may have had no choice, Dorothy did. She muffed it the first time when Allen ran off to the Army because Mamma threatened suicide. That should have warned her away from Allen immediately. What kind of husband will a man make if he joins the Army every time one of the women around the house threatens to put her head in the oven?

But Dorothy isn't thinking ahead to marriage; she is too absorbed in playing the huntress. No wonder she is divorced. Refusing to drop her sights from Allen, she writes that unspeakable letter and, as if that weren't bad enough, boasts about it to *Cosmopolitan*.

There is still a chance to save herself, however, when Mother tells Allen, "You've got to marry that girl" and

Allen concludes that he has no choice. She should see at this critical moment that a man who will marry at his mother's command is too much of a son ever to make a husband.

By agreeing to have him, Dorothy is taking on a neurotic, possibly suicidal mother-in-law and, what is worse, one who bursts into tears over Louisa May Alcott.

Cosmopolitan closes the story of Dorothy and Allen at the altar. In the *Cosmopolitan* philosophy of life, Dorothy has had a successful safari in the mating market-place jungle and will presumably find happiness if she consults last month's article on "New Nude Lingerie" and this month's on "Ways to Beat the Holiday Blues."

It would be a disservice to young huntresses not to tell the conclusion of the story of Dorothy and Allen, which *Cosmopolitan* kept secret. When they left the altar, everything went satisfactorily for a few weeks, until one day Allen's mother announced that she wanted to move in and share their apartment.

When Dorothy protested, her mother-in-law threatened suicide and Allen ran off to Las Vegas to escape Dorothy's tears, his mother's hysteria and his own indecision. Dorothy then sat down and wrote Allen a tear-jerking letter in her Louisa May Alcott style, pleading with him not to abandon both his wife and his mamma, who only wanted, each in her own way, to make a man of him.

Allen, who had always despised the works of Louisa May Alcott, but who could not stand the thought that he had made his mother unhappy, wrote back that he hated to have to make difficult choices and would do whatever his mother commanded.

"You've got to come home and support me and Dorothy," his mother replied. Feeling that he had no choice, Allen headed home by plane and, in flight, opened a copy of *Cosmopolitan,* where he read Dorothy's account of how he had been trapped.

When the plane stopped at St. Louis, Allen changed flights and returned to Las Vegas for a quick divorce. "I knew if I went back to Dorothy," he told a sympathetic court, "she'd haul me into the *Ladies Home Journal* for the 'Can This Marriage Be Saved?' department."

Dorothy's hunt for a third husband has been considerably hampered by a former mother-in-law who keeps bursting in when male quarry is visiting and weeping like a character by Louisa May Alcott.

JUNE
····· 9 ·····

On this day in the year 1902, the first Automat in America opened at 818 Chestnut Street, in Philadelphia. The Automat was fun, but no more so than its electronic-age descendants.

Al, Nick, Pete and Quentin went to an expensively decorated restaurant for lunch. The food was just as expensive as the decor and almost as tasty.

"The chef here isn't much," Al confided as they sat down, "but they've got the best menu writer on the East Coast. It cost them a fortune to hire him. He'd been in New York writing book-jacket blurbs for Gothic novels."

A waiter took their drink orders, distributed four menus and departed.

After studying his menu a few minutes, Nick said he was thinking of ordering the tender chunklets of milk-fed veal, lovingly dipped in the slightest hint of aromatic herb sauce and served in an iron casserole rushed fresh from the famed forges of France.

"That's a little too metallic for my literary taste," Al said. "Personally, I recommend the lumps of luscious back-fin crab meat delicately wrapped in light French crepes to retain the sealed-in flavors and savory juices, baked and covered with sauce Mornay in a delightful sprinkling of Parmesan cheese redolent with memories of sunny Naples."

Pete said he was watching his weight but found it hard to resist the refulgent green lightness of gelatin quivering on an emerald bed of crisp crunchy lettuce born of the mating between sparkling sunshine and cool, clear water in the golden valleys of old California.

Quentin said he didn't see anything on the menu that didn't need editing, and thought he would just have a hamburger, medium rare.

"You can't just ask for a hamburger in a place like this," Al whispered.

"The author would be insulted," said Nick.

"In France, where food really counts for something," said Pete, "men have been shot for less."

"I want a hamburger!" insisted Quentin, who tended to stubbornness. "Medium rare."

"Quent, old boy," said Al, "why not try the Seafood Symphony?"

"Because," said Quentin, "I don't want succulently clustered clumps of crab meat, jumbo shrimp, tender lobster meat and fresh salt-water fish sautéed in butter with mushrooms and shallots, blended with thick luscious cream and flavored with shimmeringly shadowed sherry wine to create a symphony in seafood, served in casserole."

The waiter, noting tensions at the table, eased within eavesdropping range.

"Have a Cowpuncher's Dream," urged Nick.

"No steaks," said Quentin.

The waiter, who had overheard, came over. He was miffed.

"Our writers do not traffic in steak," he said. "Steak is for illiterates."

This put Quentin's back up. "I demand to see the author," he said.

An overpaid man stuffed with succulent juicy adjectives presented himself. "Hamburger?" he repeated.

"Hamburger," said Quentin. "Medium rare."

The writer wandered to the water cooler, washed his hands, looked up the weather report, made some unnecessary phone calls, looked at his tongue in a mirror for symptoms of fatal disease and, when he had at last exhausted methods of killing time, went to his typewriter.

Returning to Quentin, he asked, "Is the creation you have in mind a magnificently seared thickness of sizzling goodness that has been reduced by grinders of rarest Toledo steel to mouth-watering palate-tantalizers of Kansas City beef beaded with rich ruby globules served on a farm-fresh roll and laced lavishly with great oozing lashings of rarest mustards and onions from faraway Spain?"

"Enough! Enough! Stop!" cried Quentin. "I can't listen to another bite."

The menu writer smiled in triumph and left. The waiter returned. "Are you gentlemen ready to order?" he asked.

"Yes," said Al. "Four coffees."

"And," said Nick, "send our compliments to the author."

MISERY, SECURITY AND HAPPINESS (4)

Misery is taking your wife to the spaghetti house where you used to go before you were married and discovering that you are twenty years older than any other couple in the house.

Security is arriving in a hotel lobby with "French Line" stickers on your luggage.

Happiness is when you go to a reception and it is so crowded that you can sneak in without having to go through the receiving line.

JUNE
····· 16 ·····

On this day in 1904, Leopold Bloom, after breakfasting on kidney, slightly burned, set forth on a day-long Odyssey through Dublin that changed the way men have, ever since, looked at their world. Yes, James Joyce persuaded us, Ulysses might very well have had a cake of lemon soap in his pocket throughout the whole journey, and if he might have, who among us might not be Ulysses?

QUESTION: Having advised the President on the subjects of inflation and high interest rates, dilated upon the sundry excellences of youth, condemned the excesses of violence regardless of its perpetrators' purity of political purpose and publicly urged upon the Secretary of State a more temperate oratorical policy, what beverage did our narrator consume, in what quantity did he consume it and what emotion predominated in his breast during its consumption?

ANSWER: While drinking three cups of coffee, he looked upon his work and rejoiced in what he took to be its superb quality.

QUESTION: What fantasy picture did he ruthlessly suppress before permitting his mind to move ahead to the business at hand?

ANSWER: Briefly, he envisioned a United States of America dwelling at peace with the world while its citizenry lived harmoniously, using their ample leisure in such heartwarming pastimes as fishing, buying some peanuts and Cracker Jacks at the old ball game and going to the movies with the whole darned family to see films with "G" ratings. He imagined, moreover, a delegation of mothers, generals, students with hair of diverse lengths, Asian revolutionaries, reformed street muggers and grateful women of infinite desirability thanking him, our narrator, for bringing to the Presidency that wisdom and penetrating intelligence that had assured mankind that the present era would be known in history books for evermore as "The Golden American Century."

QUESTION: What was the business at hand that compelled our narrator to suppress so rapidly this delightful fantasy?

ANSWER: It was time for our narrator to impart to us, his audience, more of the solace, insight, wisdom, intelligence and searing etcetera that, if but absorbed into the public policy, might very well, he was quite certain, have improved the quality of Western civilization in the manner aforementioned.

QUESTION: Describe the preparations he made for that impartation.

ANSWER: After seating himself adjacent to a typewriter, he cleaned his fingernails, removed a quantity of wax from his ears, telephoned a mechanized voice to ascertain the precise time, browsed through three girdle advertisements in the morning newspaper, worried about the possibility of a dear and close relative's failing algebra, removed a dangling label from his necktie, washed his bifocals with soap and warm water, observed a severe electrical storm at the window, speculated unpleasantly upon what it would feel like to be struck by lightning and, simultaneously with many of the preceding events, chewed into tiny splinters thirty-one Stim-U-Dent interdental stimulators, or toothpicks, which, he was severely displeased to recall, had only recently been raised in price by 20 percent.

QUESTION: These preparations concluded, did our narrator activate the typewriter, thus beginning the impartation process?

ANSWER: No.

QUESTION: What urgent impulse accounted for his failure thus to act?

ANSWER: He suddenly remembered the importance of informing a fellow worker of an arresting conclusion he had reached the previous night; to wit, that it seemed highly unlikely that the Washington Redskins football team would succeed at a majority of its labors during the coming autumn unless improbable improvements occurred in the quality of its offensive linemen.

QUESTION: Having made his fellow worker privy to this conclusion, stepped outside to the drugstore to purchase chewing gum, given in to a bout of self-pity about his chronic inability to keep grease stains off his clothes and holes out of his trousers, and having then resumed his place adjacent to the typewriter, for whom did our narrator very briefly feel an uncharacteristic sorrow?

ANSWER: He felt sorrow for the President of the United States, a sorrow occasioned by the realization that the President could not step out for some chewing gum during interludes when the Presidential brain went absolutely blank.

QUESTION: What kindly resolution did he make as a result of this momentary twinge of sorrow?

ANSWER: He resolved that he would not, that day, take the President publicly to task for mistakes that he, our narrator, could never possibly have made.

QUESTION: Did he believe that a grateful nation, touched by this extraordinary act of mercy for its President, would award him, out of gratitude, a citation, in ceremonies in the White House rose garden, that would be reported on network television?

ANSWER: He was persuaded that his country would not recognize his true value until after his death, and he took such satisfaction as he could from the thought that though in life he could from time to time spare Presidents, it would be impossible in his posthumous condition to prevent school teachers centuries hence from forcing his impartations, along with the sweet Shakespeare's, upon untold generations of resentful children.

QUESTION: What positive actions resulted from this cruel thought?

ANSWER: (1) The chewing into tiny splinters of a thirty-second Stim-U-Dent interdental stimulator. (2) The activation of the facial muscles required to produce a small but exceedingly pleased smile.

....

THE AMERICAN'S CREED

I believe in the interstate highway system of America as a Government of the traffic, by the traffic, for the traffic; whose rights of way are derived from the Federal gasoline tax; a limited-access automopolis in a megalopolis; a perfect asphalt, one and inseparable through the binding union of cloverleaf interchanges; established upon those principles of high-speed motoring, freedom from stop lights and justice for the trucking industry, for which Americans have sacrificed their farms, forests, streams, cities and freedom from carbon monoxide.

I therefore believe it is my duty to my interstate highway system to drive it; to support its licensed hamburger concessionaires; to stay off its median strip; to respect its passing lane; and to defend it against all enemies who seek to prevent its extension through their living rooms.

JUNE
·····20·····

All across America this month persons creaky with middle age have been saying farewell to elementary school, and their thoughts have run along lines that evoke sympathetic resonances in every parent who has ever seen his child graduate from the sixth grade.

Farewell, Ben W. Murch Elementary School. Our paths now part after twelve long years of struggle and trial. Let our names be stricken from the rolls of the P.T.A., for we have done our duty and would rest.

Twelve years ago we came to you, Ben W. Murch Elementary School, with Barbara, our eldest, and you helped us to teach her the multiplication tables; to awaken her to the excitement of the world of Dick, Jane, Sally and Spot; and, with the splendid assistance of Officer Kelly, to persuade her of the wisdom of crossing streets at guarded intersections.

As the years passed and we sent you young Charles, you put us in touch with the school psychologist, and in time we stood proud in the June sunlight and saw you send them both forth into the great world of the Alice Deal Junior High School.

And now, little Michael, our last, prepares to go forth in their footsteps. As we stand proud in the June sunlight to see you consign him to the future, our sense of sadness —evoked by this evidence that after forty years our elementary-school days are finally ended—will be tempered with exhilaration.

No longer will the call for lunch-mothers be heard on the phone. Never again will we be called upon to man the penny-pitch concession at the annual school fair. No more shall we be summoned to conference with Miss Plimpton to justify our failure to produce offspring capable of mastering the nine-times table.

Farewell, Miss Kaufman, princess among principals. How we shall miss your speeches of gratitude on behalf of the boys and girls for our annual appearance in the audience at the Ben W. Murch school play!

Farewell, Mrs. Wechsler, Mrs. Rose, Mrs. Rich, Mrs. Bode, Miss Cotter, Miss Vail, Mrs. Grieb, and all the others, some retired, some dead perhaps, with whom we have toiled a dozen years in uneasy partnership. When our patience seemed strained by your tight-fisted ways with the "A's," it was not because we were angry with your inability to perceive the brilliance of Barbara, Charles and little Michael.

No. It was because, having told the children that education was not a business of getting grades, our patience was exhausted by the labor of trying to get good grades for them. Teachers of Ben W. Murch Elementary School, have you ever at the age of thirty-nine written a book report on *Bill and Pete Visit the Zoo* and had it sent home by a second-grade teacher with a "C-minus"?

These have been years full of the exciting discovery that we are never too old to learn. Thanks to you, Ben W. Murch Elementary School, we have learned in the high afternoon of life to subtract in base eight, to recognize an adverbial phrase and to distinguish the subject of a sentence from the predicate. (The predicate has two lines drawn under it; the subject, only one.)

After twelve years with the *Weekly Reader,* we have learned who Robert Mugabe is, and Eisaku Sato, Lopez Portillo, Pol Pot, Lon Nol and Ayatollah Beheshti. Some day, perhaps, when Barbara, Charles and little Michael have all finished college, they will come for a family reunion and we will amuse ourselves by trying to guess what became of these men whose identities we spent our youths trying to master.

As we part forever, Ben W. Murch Elementary School,

the sense of relief on your part is understandable, and so it is only fair that you should indulge us in a small display of sentimentality.

We, who are now getting on toward the ultimate abyss, have been in elementary school for more than one-third of our lives. The smell of chalk dust, the sound of dodge ball, the memory of Fire Prevention Week, the sight of school-patrol badges, the passion of class elections and the excitement of the fifth-grade play have become part of our lives.

From Miss Broadbent at P.S. Number 8 in Belleville, New Jersey, back in 1931, to Miss Kaufman, the pillar of strength at Ben W. Murch, there have been more schoolmarms than lovers in our lives. Now it is all over, and it is a little sad and quite a bit shocking. Sad to discover that after all these years we have finally graduated; shocking to discover that by the time you at last get out of elementary school, you are too thick of waist, short of wind, weak of eye and faint of heart to enjoy the new freedom. Wherefore, let us satisfy ourselves with a tear.

Farewell, Ben W. Murch Elementary School.

Farewell, Childhood.

....

Eventually America will run smack into the problem problem. The essence of the problem problem can be summarized in the question, What are we going to do when the problems run out?

A Congress without any problems on its hands is like a

barber with a bald-headed clientele; its problem is a lack of problems. The barber may solve his problem problem by persuading his customers that they have "a scalp problem," which requires repeated applications of hot towels, oil swaths and follicle fertilizers. Success depends upon persuading the customer that a natural physical state, baldness, is not a natural physical state at all, but a problem, for an American faced with a problem cannot resist the urge to try solving it.

If, however, the barber says, "You have a scalp problem," and the customer replies, "Nonsense, I've simply gone bald," the barber is in trouble. A man who accepts the fact that in this world a certain amount of baldness is inevitable—even quite natural—is a menace, for he can reduce the national problem supply overnight.

If such people proliferated, we would never be able to solve our way to the really dreadful problems that can be ours if everybody will just keep insisting that the trouble with living is, it's a problem.

···········

Family solvency is not a felony, but many economists consider it vaguely unpatriotic.

···········

ENGLISH (3)

In the English language it is easy to "sit still," but impossible to "sit loud." It is no problem at all for an English speaker to "sit tight," but ask him to "sit loose" and he will go to pieces.

JUNE

..... 26 .....

This is the first weekend of the good old summertime.

"What is the meaning of summer, Daddy?" asked little Virginia, as she cuddled on her father's lap and patted his cheek with a tiny hand that was glutinous with melted chocolate.

"Summer, Virginia, is the high holiday of the American spirit," her father said. "It is a place by the seashore, a house in the hills. It is fireworks and the flag and a can of beer in a pickup truck on the turnpike. It is me holding your hand and you holding mine, and me being your tootsie-wootsie, because you see, Virginia, it's the good old summertime."

Virginia recognized in her father's simpering reply to her fatuous question the symptoms of another onset of loquacity to which he had become much given in his declining years, and she thought to deter him by changing the subject. "Can I have three dollars to go to the movies, Daddy?" she asked.

But her father was not to be stopped. "Yes, Virginia, there is a good old summertime," he said, reaching for his third gin-and-tonic, "and don't let anyone ever tell you there isn't. Summer is as big as all America. It is as tangible as an empty ice-cube tray, as romantic as heat lightning on an August night, and as dramatic as a gas station stickup.

"Summer is the croak of a bullfrog from a polluted pond, the crack of a bat on a policeman's skull, the whine of a blowout on the New Jersey Turnpike and the plop of a chocolate ice cream cone on a father's lap.

"No good old summertime? You might as well say that there are no good television repeats, no sand in the sheets, no second-degree sunburn. Summer is a wilted collar on the neck, steam on the eyeglasses, poison ivy between the toes and a mosquito bite behind the ear.

"And that's not all summer is. Summer is also a lightning bug glimmering against the sycamore, and don't you ever forget it, Virginia. A lightning bug against the sycamore, ants in the kitchen, a mole in the lawn, a snake in the meadow and a shark in the surf.

"No shark in the surf? You might as well say that there are no torsos boiled on a crowded beach, no commuters roasted in a rush-hour bus, no sirloin cremated on a backyard grill, no Mommy and Daddy fried on gin-and-tonic.

"There will always be a shark in the surf, just as there will always be black spot on the roses, crab grass in the lawn, mold in the cellar, skunk cabbage in the petunia patch and gnats in the eardrum.

"Go out to Coney if you want to understand summertime, Virginia, because summertime is when the livin' is queasy."

Virginia, who had become sleepy, yawned. "I don't care what summer is, Daddy," she said struggling to escape to bed.

"You should care," her father said. "All little girls should care what summer is, and I'm going to tell you what summer is whether you like it or not.

"Summer is a nail puncture in a bare foot, a fishhook in the back of the neck and a lawn-mower blade in the big toe. Do you know how to tell when it's summer, Virginia? When the air conditioner breaks down, that's how. When the New York Mets are in last place, that's when you know it's summer.

"When the radiator is boiling and the picnic is floating away in the thunderstorm and the roof of the seaside cottage is leaking, then do men sing, 'Sumer is icumen in, coo-coo.'

"And what kind of people would Americans be if there were no summer, Virginia? They would be a people without rose thorns in their index fingers, a people without perspiration stains on their car upholstery. They would never know the agony of a lemonade stomach-ache nor the delirium of heat prostration in the flower bed.

"There would be no mustard stains on their under-shirts. They would not remember the things they did last summer all winter long. They would not meet their love in Avalon, and the ninety-seven-pound weaklings among them would never have sand kicked in their faces by beach bullies and, hence, would do nothing to improve their scrawny physiques.

"No good old summertime, Virginia? Hah! You might as well say there is no such thing as a worm in the tomato or suntan oil in the salad, no such things as—"

But Virginia had gone to sleep, and so had Virginia's mother, and the only listener still awake was a mosquito who was happily stitching a row of small bites around the wrist of Virginia's father.

·············

ENGLISH (4)

The English language makes it easy to go to places like "pieces" without making a move. Through the miracle of English, a man can "go to pieces," "go to seed," "go to pot" and "go to the dogs" simply by sitting in a deep chair with a bottle.

JULY

SUMMERTIME: lightning and hollyhocks. Smack of baseball against leather. Country sounds in thick balmy night, and night sound of trains miles away, that long-ago sound. Not too long ago you could still cross the country by train, feel the unity of mountain and plain, desert and lake, sense the continuity of present with past. In the predawn black, with bunk swaying like a ship in rough seas, you could hear the whistle warn prairie towns of its coming, feel the riot subside in your bones, listen to the brakes squeal as the train slowed for no-where junction, sense that you were part of a continent, a link with the past. Summer . . . thunderstorms and sentimentality, high corn and blood hate . . .

JULY
······ 4 ······

In the past this has been a good day for getting a revolution launched. Why not test the magic again today? Usually a revolution starts with a middle-class man sitting in a jail cell, writing. One day his message goes out through the bars, and old tyrannies collapse. What? You say you have no message? Are you quite certain about that? Think a moment . . .

For twenty years Harry had trained himself to love the Organization and to walk abruptly out of any gathering at which the tiniest mouse of un-Organization thought appeared. He had always praised General Motors and the F.B.I., and his favorite toast was, "My Organization —right or wrong!"

Before marriage, he had had his chosen bride investigated and certified both loyal and presentable by the Organization. His children were sent to schools that taught the Organization way of life.

And so, when Harry noted one day that he was being tailed by men in squeaky shoes, he immediately went to the Office of Organization Security for an explanation. To an inscrutable man with hooded eyes, he said, "Surely the Organization, which is the most awesome combine of inhuman forces ever merged into a single insuperable force on this earth, can have nothing to fear from one miserable little human being like me."

"Keep talking," said the functionary.

"I have never bent, spindled or folded," said Harry. "I believe that bombs are peace. I hold these truths to be self-evident: That man is endowed by the Organization with certain inalienable rights, and among these are expressways, television and the pursuit of credit."

"Are you now, or have you ever been, an associate of anyone, male or female, who wears a beard, jeans, a turtleneck sweater or refuses to observe the Organization creed of cleanliness?"

"On my honor," said Harry, "I never speak to anyone whose skin is not soaped twice a day or whose throat, mouth, teeth and armpits are not gargled, washed, brushed or sprayed with chemicals."

"Do you believe in the new washday miracle?"

"Of course," said Harry. "And in heartier flavor, more pleasure, crispier goodness and faster relief, as well."

The inscrutable man sighed. "You know, of course," he said, "that you are not entitled to an explanation of why you are being investigated." Harry nodded.

"The Organization cannot tell you," the man went on, "because the Organization's mission is solely to help people, and there are a great many people, my friend. A great many people."

"But I'm people, too," said Harry.

"Correction. You are a person. The Organization never finds it necessary to investigate people. The Organization *is* people. The Organization loves people. The enemy of people, and therefore of the Organization, is the person. Like yourself."

Harry blanched. "Are there a great many persons?" he asked.

"Far too many still," said the inscrutable man, "though we are gradually wearing them down. They form committees to stop the Organization from pouring asphalt over their houses so that people can drive faster. They refuse to have zip code numbers tattooed on their brains so that advertisers can send people their junk mail more cheaply. They go about the world raising questions about General Motors' cars and the Organization's policies."

"I don't suppose," said Harry, "that there is much future in being a person."

The inscrutable man chuckled all too scrutably. "Offhand," he said, "how many Person's Republics can you think of in the world?"

When Harry arrived home he told his wife, "It's no use. I'm a person and I have to be ground down." And then he had a wild idea.

"Listen," he said, "let's cut out. We'll take all the

credit cards and see how far we can run before we're caught. We can probably make it to the isles of Greece before the machines catch us, and it'll be cheaper for the Organization to leave us there than bring us back here."

Harry's wife, who for years had been a volunteer agent for the Organization's gumshoe force, immediately made a telephone call. "You are quite right," said the party at the far end of the line. "If he runs like that, the Organization will cut off your insurance, foreclose the mortgage, cancel his pension and hold the entire family up to public ridicule. Put the restraints on him at once!"

Nowadays Harry sits in his office writing messages on scrap paper and sailing them out the window. They all say, "Help! I am a person!" No one ever comes to help, of course. Who in this world could take such a message seriously?

JULY

····· 5 ·····

He is famous for having said that there is a sucker born every minute and for the circus, and, so, he was that rarest of men—the philosopher-showman. As such, he was the father of Madison Avenue. His name

was P. T. (for Phineas Taylor) Barnum. He was born July 5, 1810.

The American press responded with considerable amusement some years ago when the Duke of Edinburgh was assigned the company of a Hollywood public-relations man to help him through an eleven-day visit to the United States. There was no reason for amusement, of course, because the incident was not without precedent in the chronicles of British royalty.

As a matter of fact, the first person of any consequence to interest himself in the science of public relations was King Henry VIII of England. In the year 1537, deeply worried about his image and about polls showing a six-point drop in his popularity since the beheading of Anne Boleyn, Henry retained the then obscure Gorbaduc Beaulieu as Steward of Royal Relations with the Public, or Publick, as it was then called.

It was a stormy and short-lived relationship. Gorbaduc Beaulieu, who has rightfully been called "the father of public relations," was centuries ahead of his time. The transcript of his first conference with Henry VIII reveals the sort of difficulty he was to encounter to the end.

"Good Beaulieu," said the King, "we extend to thee warm welcome to our presence."

To which Beaulieu gave the immortal reply, "Rex, my friends call me Gorbaduc." This was evidently accompanied by a hearty clap on the royal back, for Henry replied, "Rogue! would'st lay violent hands on our scapula?"

It was the King's stuffy refusal to open his mind to the new science that made it almost impossible for Gorbaduc to do anything for his image. For example, after a penetrating analysis of Henry's image problem, Gorbaduc drew up his far-seeing show-the-crown campaign, only to see Henry tear it up in a fearful display of temper at Westminster Hall.

"We've got to get the crown out of the palace and away from the Tower chopping block and humanize it," Gorbaduc said. "When the public thinks of the King nowadays, what does it think of? Divorces, head chopping, fights with the Pope. Our task is to show that, underneath it all, the King is a regular fellow."

Thus, Gorbaduc proposed that Henry start paying surprise visits to slum neighborhoods and engaging in impromptu cricket games with disadvantaged children. Henry did. Once, dashing off to Islington where a huge crowd of photographers, reporters and disadvantaged urchins had been assembled by Gorbaduc, he played ten minutes of cricket on a sticky wicket.

Unfortunately, years of soft living had destroyed the King's figure and left him short of wind, and the ludicrous figure he cut was heightened when he was hit in the crown while trying to catch a fly ball. He withdrew in a rage calling for Gorbaduc's head.

Still undiscouraged, Gorbaduc tried to persuade the King to get into shape. "You are eating too much boar," he pointed out in a violent conference one afternoon. "It's not only bad for your waistline, it's worse for your image."

Gorbaduc noted that market analysis showed the man in the street regarded the country's handful of boar eaters as remote, snobbish and aristocratic. He urged Henry to make frequent appearance in Soho and Fleet Street and to eat fish and chips with the people.

Henry agreed to try. He let Gorbaduc persuade him to shave off his beard, leave his osprey-plumed hat at home and put on a rumpled old doublet that looked as if it had been slept in. Then, surrounded by photographers, he strolled up to a fish-and-chips stand in Piccadilly Circus and bought a shilling's worth of fried plaice, greasy potatoes, salt, pepper and vinegar, served in an old newspaper.

Unfortunately, the woman who ran the stand had failed to recognize Henry without his beard and osprey plumes, and, hence, had taken no unusual pains in the kitchen. For three days Henry, violently ill, cried feverishly for Gorbaduc's head.

When the King recovered, Gorbaduc proposed filming *The Henry VIII Story.* It was to be a musical, based on Henry's youthful career as a ballad writer. By taking slight artistic liberties, it would show that Henry, now in his middle years, still yearned to escape the kingship and devote his time to writing musicals for the West End theatre. Don Ameche and Alice Faye had agreed to star.

"This is ridiculous," Henry said, as he finished the script and called for his headsman.

"Hank, baby, you are making a big mistake," were Gorbaduc's last prophetic words from the block. Sure enough, four hundred years later, the Henry VIII story was filmed with Charles Laughton, which is why we all think of Henry nowadays as an overweight boar eater, who never played cricket with poor disadvantaged kids or ate fish and chips with the folks.

Fortunately for our leaders of today, they have all learned Gorbaduc's lesson.

············

Without Congress we would have no way to put off until 1989 what we can do tomorrow.

JULY
⋯⋯ 20 ⋯⋯

On this day in 1969 man first set foot on ground that was not earth. On our way to wherever it is we are going, we had reached the moon. There was nobody there—at least nobody recognizable—but one day, we knew, we would arrive someplace where there would be—well, *something.* . . .

It is a statistical probability that somewhere in the cosmos there lies a planet teeming with life. That this life will take the form of people is, on the other hand, extremely improbable. More likely it will consist of helks.

Now the awkward thing about helks is that it is very difficult for people to communicate with them. This is because helks do not talk. Instead, they smeen. When a talking human being confronts a smeening helk, the result is apt to be frustration.

"For heaven's sake, quit smeening and speak up," the earth person will demand. And the uncomprehending helk will respond by smeening something utterly unintelligible.

Anyone who has ever gone to the zoo and tried to communicate with a hippopotamus knows the problem. It is simply impossible to get a word of sense out of a hippopotamus. The hippopotamus undoubtedly feels the same way about the human being. The consequence is that relations between human beings and hippopotamuses tend to be meaningless.

In view of all this, it is difficult to understand all those people who are reluctant to concede that there can be no life on Mars. If there were life on Mars, it would consist of things like jerns and obglots; and people who have not even learned to develop a meaningful relationship with the hippopotamus can scarcely be expected to do much with either a jern, which is a mischievous form of moss, or an obglot, which is just what it sounds like.

On balance, it must be considered good news that

Mars contains neither jerns, obglots or any other form of life. If it did, the Government would be forced to spend millions on projects to communicate with them, and the result probably would be the discovery that jerns and obglots are even denser than the hippopotamus.

In the end it would come down to going to the zoo once a year and watching the obglot scratch itself, which is not much return for the money involved in discovering it, failing to communicate with it and crating it back from Mars.

The helks, which still remain to be discovered in the deep cosmos, are another matter. The ugly fact is that we know precious little about helks. (For that matter, they may not even be helks; they may be gwergs, but never mind that.) Assume for the moment that billions have been spent in the search for a little companionship in the universe, and the first earth crew lands on a planet swarming with helks.

The first question is whether the crew would recognize a helk. A helk, for all we know, may very well cover hundreds of square miles and look like a dead lunar landscape. Even assuming the best—that a helk looks somewhat like a hippopotamus—the futility of addressing it will immediately be evident to the crew.

"Take us to the head helk" can sound pretty silly when addressed to several hundred miles of dead lunar landscape, or even to a distorted hippopotamus. When the result is nothing more rewarding than a lot of incomprehensible smeening, the crew is likely to wonder whether its trip has really been worthwhile.

Some people, of course, fancy that the helks will bear a sensible resemblance to man, will speak English, or at least French, and have the sensibility to invite the crew to a banquet with helk dancing girls and brilliant helk leaders, who will unravel the deepest mysteries of the universe while serving the finest burgundy.

Merely to state the proposition is to betray the dangers inherent in this, mercifully, unlikely possibility. Reverse the situation, and imagine that the helks, hungry for companionship in the universe, have landed a crew on earth. "They are remarkably like people," the papers will report.

"That means they are up to no good" is the thought that will flash through a million minds. "With all our problems, do we really need more people, especially since they call themselves helks?" is the question that will be asked in a hundred chanceries. The odds of those helks ever being allowed to report back to the home planet would not be good.

Fortunately, we can probably rely on the helks being more like a dead lunar landscape or a distorted hippopotamus when they are eventually discovered. They will smeen idiotically instead of speaking decent English.

"What is it like, this strange life on other planets?" the reporters will ask the returning astronauts. "It's like trying to talk to a hippopotamus," the astronauts will say.

"Fun on a hot Sunday afternoon, but you know nothing interesting can ever come of it."

And then Congress will appropriate another billion to make contact with the mysterious gwerg.

....

The sinister nature of the American soil is apparent in places like Gettysburg. Fertilize it with the blood of heroes, and it brings forth a frozen-custard stand.

JULY
······ 31 ······

If you are like most Americans, you have either just ended or are just beginning the best part of the year.

EXCERPTS FROM A VACATIONER'S DIARY

SATURDAY   Arrived exhausted and trembling after fourteen-hour drive. This house is named "Mare's Nest" and has a library consisting of every *National Geographic* published up to 1938, a complete set of the *Bobbsey Twins*, two novels by Marie Corelli and a copy of *Beau Geste*.

The children have gone to bed in a state of shock. Reason: No television set. Bambi wants to go home first thing tomorrow. Little Archie says, "I feel like I've been amputated."

SUNDAY   A forty-eight-hour day of rain. Am bitten by a spider.

MONDAY   Rain continues like an all-day bombardment. Buy the children a radio to give them some noise. It seems to soothe them a little, but not much. Josette flies into a rage upon being refused permission to use the car and bites Rover. Bed sheets are damp. Mold growing on the carpets. Read *The Bobbsey Twins Go to the Seashore* and seventeen issues of the *National Geographic,* and pray for sunshine.

TUESDAY   Sunshine! Glorious sunshine! Everyone rushes to the beach, soaks up four hours of sun. Have just returned from Dr. Vetch's for treatment of acute sunburn. "Stay out of the sun for at least a week," he warns. "What am I going to do?" I ask. "Drop by my house," he says, "and I'll lend you some back copies of the *National Geographic* to help pass the time."

WEDNESDAY   Sneak into town and buy a copy of *Playboy.*

THURSDAY   Josette bends the car around the fence post trying to get out of the yard. Damage: About $150.

FRIDAY   Every fuse in "Mare's Nest" blows out at 8:10 P.M. Conduct a two-hour search for the fuse box and finally locate it in a secret chamber under the back porch. Strike head on nail-studded rafter and have to visit Dr. Vetch for tetanus injection.

SATURDAY   Finally solve mystery of why Bambi, Josette and little Archie have been so serene the past few days. They have found a friend with a television set and are sneaking off to his house to mainline big injections of "General Hospital" and "Laverne and Shirley." In a most effective lecture, tell them I feel the purity of our vacation has been violated. Bambi and little Archie promise not to do it again. Josette demands permission to take the car and drive home.

SUNDAY   Rain. Play "Go Fish" for six hours with children.

MONDAY   Finish the last *National Geographic* in the library. Josette loses the car key at the beach. Little Archie undertakes to fix the antique grandfather's clock on the stairway, and it now strikes fifty-two times every fifteen minutes.

TUESDAY   Carried to Dr. Vetch's by ambulance for eight stitches in scalp after being struck by an escaped surfboard while floating in the water off the south shore.

WEDNESDAY   The clock repairman comes and for $149 restores things temporarily to working order. Since 7 P.M., however, the clock has been striking 208 times every hour.

THURSDAY   Our neighbors in "Heathcliff's Nightmare" complain to the police that our clock is keeping them awake. The clock man promises to take it away and replace it with an even more antique clock for $1,335. Little Archie got up on the roof this afternoon and kicked off half the shingles on the east end of "Mare's Nest."

FRIDAY   Awakened at 3 A.M. today by a sense of dampness about the feet and found the lower half of the bed afloat as a result of heavy rain pouring in through the damaged roof. Developed a fever of 103 about noon, and Dr. Vetch urged going into the hospital as a precaution against pneumonia. Refused when he told me the hospital had just gotten the latest issue of the *National Geographic.*

SATURDAY   Roofers came today. Felt so much better I decided to treat everybody to a lobster dinner. Price of lobster: $5 a pound. With cutting wit, told fish dealer, "In that case maybe I'd better have the chinchilla." "We don't have none," he said. Concluded that he was too oafish to get the point, but discovered on arrival back at "Mare's Nest" that he had unpegged the cutting claw of a three-pounder. Visited Dr. Vetch for treatment of severely jagged laceration of the right index finger while preparing dinner.

SUNDAY   Leaving "Mare's Nest" for home within the hour. Have not felt so good for a year. Children have never been happier. Dr. Vetch just dropped in to say good-by, but as the clock was striking the hour it was impossible to converse. Sensed, however, that he was genuinely going to miss me, and in a moment of emotion handed him my copy of *Playboy.* He seemed as delighted to get it as I was to see the end of another vacation.

In the heyday of Hollywood a trip to the movies was undertaken in much the same spirit as a trip to Coney Island. At the neighborhood houses you could see a double feature for ten cents in 1933 and twenty-five cents in 1941. Downtown, where admissions went as high as fifty cents, the theaters were of a plush vulgarity so obviously inimical to culture that the exhibitors could have screened the works of Giotto without making the audience feel uneasy.

Now, however, when we are clearly on notice that movies are culture and that what we are seeing is cinema, the knowledge that we may be in the presence of art shackles us and makes it hard for us to react honestly. In the old Roxy, when it was bad, you said, "It's a piece of cheese." In the new cinema you mutter, "It's a cultural experience," and change the subject.

············

INSIDE FACTS ABOUT PROGRESS (2)

Usually, terrible things that are done with the excuse that progress requires them are not really progress at all, but just terrible things.

············

DREADFUL DISEASE

Sociologists agree that the worst thing that can happen to an American child nowadays is youth. When the malady strikes it may help a little for the parent to take his child aside and gently explain that while youth is indeed a terrible affliction, every case in history has been cured—and that the cure is usually worse than the ailment.

AUGUST

THE SMOG has been sitting here for four or five days. It creates beautiful orange-lozenge moonrises, but it also makes the eyes smart. Moving about with the feel of it against the skin is like wearing dirty laundry, but those responsible for the public safety say that this is not a dangerous onset and that the wind from the west will soon bring relief.

AUGUST

····· 6 ·····

On this day in 1945 the first nuclear bomb ever dropped in anger killed for certain 78,150 persons, injured 37,425 persons and left 13,083 persons "missing" in Hiroshima and set off a race which we are still running.

A mean man on a mean horse rode meanly into town. He was no stranger.

"It's the Mean Kid," the boys in the saloon whispered when he strode to the bar. Then everybody shut up, including the piano player. They knew the Kid hated to have people talking and playing the piano when he was drinking. It interfered with his thinking about the fellow he'd come to town to gun.

Outside in the street there was a lot of dust and a pretty widder and buckboards and clean, decent folks who were tired of lawlessness. Through the dust you could hear ominous background music. "Killin' music," the town folks called it. "Seems like we never have no tension in this town without that background music whinin' through the dust," a clean, decent feed merchant had once said.

"The Kid's in town, Luke," a deputy told a lean man with good jaw muscles. The man's name was Luke. Sometimes he wore a star. Nights he sat around the jail humming to himself because he was too shy to talk to girls.

"I'll go on up there to the saloon and see what kind of guns the Kid's packin'," said the deputy. Outside, the tumbleweeds were tumbling through the half-finished schoolhouse where Luke hoped he'd some day have children of his own learning to do sums on their slates if he ever got up his nerve to ask a girl for a date.

The jail door opened shyly. It was a shy girl from back East—Boston, in fact. She had come West with her fancy Radcliffe corsets and education for reasons that made no sense whatever to Luke. For months she had been giving the whole town a pain with her fancy Boston accent and sidesaddle riding.

"This killing has got to stop, Luke," she pleaded. "Killing, killing, killing—that's all you know out here." Luke thought she looked just like a high-spirited filly, and he wanted to kiss her but he didn't know how.

"There won't be any killin'," he hummed, "as long as I've got enough guns to keep all these visitin' Kids from thinkin' they can kill and get away with it."

As the girl from back East was led away to a boarding

house, the deputy returned. "The Kid says he's gonna be walkin' down the street at tea time a-packin' two six-guns," he told Luke.

"You go on back up there and tell the Kid," said Luke, "that I'll be walkin', too. With two six-guns and a sawed-off Winchester."

At the saloon, the Kid was passing the time by scaring the daylights out of the bartender. "Two six-guns and a sawed-off Winchester," he mused. "That cuts it! You there!" He pointed to a craven coward. "Go down to the mine and get me a passel of dynamite."

And, turning to the deputy, "You tell Luke I'll be walkin' down the street at dinner time a-packin' two six-guns, a sawed-off Winchester and a passel of dyna-mite."

"Get all the dynamite you can lay hands on," Luke told the deputy, "and wheel up those two cannon the Army forgot down at the depot. Then tell the Kid I'll be waitin' for him with two six-guns, a sawed-off Winchester, all the dynamite I can lay hands on and two cannon."

Back at the saloon, that called for another drink. "Can't anybody turn off that background music?" the Kid demanded, but nobody could. Then the Kid consulted the mail-order catalogue. "Tell Luke," he instructed the deputy, "that I'll be walkin' down the street at high noon two months from now a-packin' two six-guns, a sawed-off Winchester, a passel of dynamite, two cannon and a bomb big enough to blow this whole town off the map."

Luke raised. "Two six-guns, a sawed-off Winchester, all the dynamite I can lay hands on, two cannon, a bomb big enough to blow this whole town off the map and another bomb that can explode the Kid's bomb in mid-air with enough bang to blow the whole state off the map," Luke said.

The Kid, who needed a shave by this time, went back to his mail-order catalogue. Meanwhile, back at the schoolhouse, the girl from back East was rallying the town folks and the buckboards. "The way I see it," she said, to loud applause, "what this town needs is just a little more killin'."

That night the crowd seized Luke and the Kid as they dozed on carpets of bullets, but just before they could begin the lynching the authorities galloped up, snatched both men from the noose and rushed them away to a lunatic asylum.

AUGUST

···· **8** ····

We can never know for certain, of course, but it must have been on just such an August day as this that Samson's hair was cut by Delilah.

The fondest dream of many an American father came true for Walter Neaterly when his son, Leroy, had his hair cut.

Walter did not immediately recognize the beautifully kempt young man who strode into his house. "Are you from the F.B.I. or the Credit Bureau?" Walter asked him, with a resignation that amounted to a plea of guilty in either case.

"Come off it, Dad," the boy said. "I'm Leroy."

He was indeed. Walter was convinced of it as soon as he heard the voice. In appearance, however, the lad was an absolute stranger. Three years earlier, at the age of sixteen, Leroy had begun to let his hair grow. In the past eighteen months the boy had affected the hair and clothing styles of Lionel Barrymore in his memorable performance as Rasputin.

Since Walter's last sight of the boy's jaw line and brow, Leroy's face had secretly become broader and fleshier behind its hairy covering. The sweet if slightly corrupt sixteen-year-old face that Walter had always associated with his son was gone. In its place was the face of an alien.

Walter did not much like it. He felt an impulse to ask, "Where have you put Leroy's face?" He restrained the impulse. After all, he reflected, this face was what he had yearned to see naked these many months past.

Leroy's jaw was beautifully shaven. His hair, trimmed to two inches at the forelock, could have passed inspection by the White House police. Walter noted for the first time that Leroy's ears were much too big for his skull, which was decidedly lopsided on account of a flat spot on its right rear quadrant.

Leroy's neatly pressed gray slacks, gray sports jacket, gray shirt and gray necktie, set off by a marvelously polished pair of gray shoes, was the wardrobe which Walter had dreamed for years of seeing on his son.

"My son," he said, trying to sound emotional, "you have made your father very happy." While he was saying this, Walter later recalled, he felt oddly unhappy. He had the most terrible sensation of not liking this Leroy very much, or, perhaps, of being threatened by him. Did he, after all, really want a son who could be mistaken for an F.B.I. man or a Credit Bureau agent?

"Yes," Leroy said, "I have cut my hair and seen the light."

"That means you no longer believe in the revolution?" Walter asked.

"As the hair was falling from my ears, the scales fell from my eyes," Leroy said. "I saw that the revolution would be bad for the system. And now that my hair is short, I can see that the system is, though not perfect, the best of all possible systems."

"And you don't want to change anything anymore?"

"Not since my haircut," Leroy said. "I want my life to be just like yours."

"And you're not going to fool around with these crazy protesters any longer?"

"With the vision that can be gained only at the barber shop," Leroy said, "I now see that it is often necessary for great powers to devastate small nations in order to keep hair short throughout the free world."

"I guess you're through with that loud music, too."

"From now on," Leroy said, "all I want to hear is Bing Crosby and the Andrews Sisters."

"No more rock festivals?" Walter asked. "No more nude bathing? No more love-ins?"

"Dad, you and Mom were right," Leroy said. "There is joy enough for everyone to be had from watching prime-time television on America's three great commercial networks."

"And you'll go to college and work hard for good grades so you can get a good job with an expense account and a gray suit and marry the kind of girl who can pass a security check by one of America's great corporations, and the two of you can have two and a half children like typical Americans, and two and a half cars, and go into heavy debt to buy the new miracle fabrics that will make you twice as sexy?"

"Thanks to my new haircut," Leroy said, "I wouldn't have life any other way. I will campaign for more cost overruns at the Pentagon, extension of the Congressional seniority system beyond the grave, greater inequity in our tax laws, and the return of tail fins on the American automobile."

"It will be just like it was in the 1950s, all over again, only more polluted," Walter said. Leroy nodded his lopsided head with the water-jug ears and excused himself to go practice his expense-account padding.

Walter says he felt inexplicably disappointed. This moment, of which he had dreamed so long, seemed merely bleak. He felt as if he had lost something precious. Could it have been a son? Walter wondered.

Since that day, Walter has not had his hair cut.

············

ENGLISH (5)

The English language makes it easy for people to denounce galleries for showing "abstract" art. This is because galleries in the English-speaking world are forbidden to show "stract" art.

AUGUST
····· 15 ·····

This is Napoleon's birthday. Celebrate it by going to one of the few places Napoleon couldn't conquer. England. Imagine, if Napoleon had gotten to England, what loot he would have brought back to stuff the Louvre!

A person can improve his understanding of antiques after a few weeks in London, particularly if he is traveling with someone determined to lead him through each of London's 1,234 miles of street markets where this precious debris of the past is sold.

At home it is relatively easy to avoid antiques by staying out of Connecticut barns and keeping a heavy foot on the gas pedal. In London, with a swarm of dusty-merchandise peddlers huddled around every other corner, there is nothing to do but plunge in. When you plunge into strange subjects, of course, you find that nothing is a total bore, and this is true even of the broken-down world of antiques.

For example, how many persons know about the event called "a great buy"? "A great buy" is to antiques what a grand-slam home run is to baseball, and antique fans talk constantly of terrific "great buys" they have heard about.

What is "a great buy"? Well, suppose you found Napoleon's hat rack in a stall in the Portobello Road and offered $3 for it, and the merchant, thinking it was a broken piece of floor board from a 1930 rumble seat, lets you have it, after haggling, for $4.50. You have made "a great buy," since Napoleon's hat rack would obviously be worth hundreds of thousands of millions of dollars to the proper buyer.

Just as obviously, Napoleon's hat rack is not found every day lying on a market stall. Nor is the Duke of Wellington's cane, nor Lucrezia Borgia's brandy snifter, nor one of Leonardo's lost portraits. For this reason, "great buys" are much rarer than grand-slam home runs. They are so rare, in fact, that nobody knows anyone who has actually scored "a great buy."

Everybody, however, has heard of somebody who knows somebody who once scored "a great buy." Six dealers in Islington alone say they have heard of persons who bought Napoleon's hat rack for mere trifles.

Considering the millions and millions of antiques that one sees in London, it is surprising how little variety there is. A fairly careful survey of several London antique markets suggests there are only eight basic items for sale.

These are (1) the broken clock; (2) the old map, usually of a place unlisted in geographies, called Novum Cloacum; (3) the incomplete set of dining-room chairs (commonly five or seven), one of which has a broken rung; (4) the set of three silver spoons; (5) the cracked demi-tasse with saucer; (6) the dining-room table with (Variation A) no leaves or (Variation B) a dangerous split in one leg; (7) the oil portrait of someone who, though unidentified, might very well be the Electress Sophia of Hanover or King Umberto the First; and (8) the first edition volume of a history of animal husbandry during the year 1703 in the environs of Dumfries.

Some of these items are, in fact, very old, but only a very slight power of observation is required to see that the great bulk must be mass-produced at a vast antique factory, a veritable Detroit of Dilapidation, capable of turning automatically cracked demi-tasses off the production line along with incomplete sets of dining-room chairs at a truly prodigious rate.

How can we justify such scandalous conjecture? Simply by counting the number of antiques available today. On a typical Saturday morning, to cite but one statistic, there are more broken clocks for sale in the Portobello Road than there were families in Western Europe during the eighteenth and nineteenth centuries combined.

When we reflect that comparable numbers of broken clocks are available at antique centers in Bermondsey, Camden Passage and Brompton Road, it becomes obvious that somebody must be turning them out at a good clip. The dealers deny it; still, there are rumors of a huge industrial center just outside Naples. . . .

One last oddity about antiques. The seller, not unnaturally, always tells the buyer that he (the buyer) will be able to sell this remarkable item—let us say the old map—at a splendid profit when he returns to the United States. The oddity is that the buyer often believes this and is perfectly capable of replying to, "You don't mean to tell me you paid $85 for that map of Novum Cloacum!" with, "That shows what you know about antiques! That map will sell for $190 back home."

Maybe it will, if you happen to have the use of a barn in Connecticut and nothing to do with your time but sit on an egg crate until a rich victim wanders in. To raise such points in an antique shop, however, is in extremely poor taste.

....

TIPS FOR LAWN CARE

Read several gardening books for advice on the best times of day to water the lawn. Watering at certain times leads to fungus and watering at other times encourages crab grass. Decide whether you prefer fungus or crab grass and water accordingly.

AUGUST
...... 19 ......

Summer's sun is a bit lower in the sky, shadows longer in the afternoon and twilight faster to arrive. The body's alarm clock sends melancholy signals; time is hastening, summer is passing, hurry up and grasp its pleasures while you may. And if you grasp them resolutely you will when school re-opens—much too soon now—be prepared to write with ease when the teacher assigns the opening-day essay: "What I Did On My Summer Vacation."

It is no laughing matter, if you have traveled eastward over the great sea to Athens, to be confronted with the Acropolis.

There it stands, that soaring rock crowned with the Parthenon. Birthplace of Western civilization, symbol of man's liberation from the ancient tyrannies of death and despotism, the place where the human spirit first learned to breathe free, where the human mind first wakened to the beauty of life. The place where it all began.

There it stands, shining in the Mediterranean sunlight, and what are you to say about it? It is the tourist's duty to say *something*. But what?

To answer this question, an agent was once assigned to mingle with tourists on the Acropolis and record what they said. The following is a representative sampling from his notes:

Father to his child: "Do you see Mamma anywhere?"

Woman to another woman while approaching the Parthenon: "Is this mountain-climbing or not? Just tell me in one word."

Man with movie camera to man with two still cameras: "There's too much traffic here to take pictures."

Man to two other men while looking at the temple on the site where the Goddess Athene fought Poseidon for possession of Athens: "It was the worst flight I've ever had. The steak came out like a rock. I said to the stewardess, 'I can't eat that steak.'"

Woman to man while looking at Parthenon: "You wonder where all these old things come from, don't you?"

Conversation between man and wife: Wife—"How are your legs holding out?" Husband—"They're killing me."

Man replying to tour guide who had just said that she never tired of looking at the Parthenon: "Just like Niagara Falls. You can go back and look at that time after time."

Woman to husband climbing steps of the Parthenon: "Now that I got you to buy those shoes in Rome, don't break a leg."

One woman to another while looking down on the ancient Athenian marketplace: "What was the name of that Danish beer?"

A tourist was overheard to say of the Parthenon: "That's really something, isn't it?" Another said, "It sure is a wreck." Another commented, "Eggplant! Eggplant! What's so civilized about a country that serves you eggplant three meals a day?"

Now, it is easy for persons sitting smugly at home to feel contempt for these tourists. In fact, they deserve nothing but sympathy. It is a terrible responsibility to be a tourist standing before the world's most celebrated treasures.

There is something about touring—perhaps the thought of all the money it is costing—that compels a man to utter words aloud about the "sight" looming before his very eyes, yet none of the guidebooks supplies him with suitable phrases to utter.

Most tourists arrive in Athens fairly late in their itineraries, perhaps after visiting Italy, Paris, London and Vienna. This means that by the time they come up against the Acropolis their limited stock of commentary has been exhausted.

In Rome they use up, "It sure makes you think, doesn't it?" while viewing the Roman Forum. "It's amazing!" is exhausted in Venice, and good old "Glorious!" is spent on Florence.

"What a town this must have been in the old days!" is worn out in Paris, and "Beautiful!" is worn threadbare by the Vienna Opera, "The Last Supper" and Parisian cooking. By the time the average tourist arrives in Athens all he has left in him for the Acropolis is a "Do you see Mamma anywhere?" or, "Just like Niagara Falls."

It is sad, really, to arrive at a place like the Acropolis, which makes the blood stir, and find that all you have left to give is, "What was the name of that Danish beer?" But how else can one respond?

There is a way without words, and it is easy. By sitting on one of Athens's rooftop gardens at night when the Acropolis is illuminated and the moon is setting behind the Parthenon, and by keeping very quiet and not thinking about the eggplant, it is possible to feel like crying. Whether with joy or despair, no one can say.

It is commonplace nowadays to discover that "the kids" about whom some broken parent has been weeping into his third martini are, in fact, women far advanced in the age of nubility and 220-pound brutes bearded like scouring pads and wiser in the ways of life than Casanova.

··············

There are no liberals behind steering wheels.

AUGUST
······ 29 ······

If this were a Presidential election year, this would be the time when the valiant few returned home to families that were not entirely prepared for what was to come.

There has been a lot of noise from Sweeney's house these past few days. Mrs. Sweeney says it is because Sweeney went to the Presidential nominating convention, and now that he is back home he cannot readjust to reality.

"Sweeney got back Saturday night," she said. "He walks into the parlor, sets down his bags, gives me and the kids the V-for-Victory salute and bawls out, 'My fellow Americans, I bring you a man who will meet the challenge without partisanship, a man who has never been found wanting, a man who has been marked by destiny,' and so on.''

Sweeney was nominating himself as a favorite-son candidate for standard bearer of the Sweeney household. After staging a twenty-minute demonstration, in which he upset the coffee table and broke the Tiffany lampshade, he started to endorse himself with four seconding speeches.

He was halfway through the third when the doctor arrived and gave him a sedative. After that, things quieted down except for an occasional bellow in the night. ''The children will clear the aisles and Mrs. Sweeney will take her seat!'' was one of those bellows. It awakened the whole neighborhood at about 4:30 A.M.

Next morning when Sweeney came down to breakfast he insisted that Mrs. Sweeney open the proceedings by singing ''The Star-Spangled Banner.'' She obliged him. The doctor had told her that Sweeney was merely suffering an onset of *conventia praecox* which, with humoring, would pass rapidly as the ordeal of his experience began to recede from memory.

''Well,'' Mrs. Sweeney says, ''after I sang the anthem he seemed more like his old self, at least until I served the egg course.''

Sweeney likes his eggs sunny side up, and that morning they were scrambled. "Madame Chairman! Madame Chairman!" Sweeney roared. "I request that the table be polled!"

Sweeney, it turned out, wanted to take a head count among the children to determine how many supported scrambled eggs and how many were for eggs sunny side up. The vote went 3 to 1 for scrambled, and Sweeney conceded that under the unit rule he had been defeated.

"Off the record," he told a neighbor over the hedge that afternoon, "there has been some erosion in my egg count this morning, but when the family sees that I'm the only man who can unify it, they'll all be with me on the first ballot."

As chance would have it, the day happened to be Sweeney's birthday, and just when it appeared that he was coming back to reality—he had turned on the TV set and settled down with the comic strips—the children presented him with a necktie.

Naturally, he had to make an acceptance speech. It lasted forty-five minutes. "Sweeney had the children in tears," Mrs. Sweeney says. "He said he'd wear that necktie from the mountains to the prairies to the oceans white with foam, through amber waves of grain, through purple-mountained majesties and across the fruited plain.

"When Sweeney said he accepted the necktie in the spirit of Abraham Lincoln, Theodore Roosevelt and those great Democrats, Jefferson, Jackson and Woodrow Wilson, even I wanted to cheer."

Later, there was a big birthday party. Sweeney seemed perfectly normal until he discovered that the Kents and the Hobcoxes were not acquainted with each other.

"It is with a feeling of utter inadequacy," he told Sam Kent, "that I stand before you tonight for the purpose of introducing a man whose achievements have long since made him an officehold name in the great and distinguished American firm of Pearson, Forbes and Auchincloss. A Montanan by birth, a true son of the land of shining mountains, he brings to his every endeavor that spirit of freshness and open air that marks him as truly a man for all seasons. And so, Sam Kent, I give you a great ad man, a patriotic martini drinker and one of the real human beings of our magnificent subdivision—Mickey Hobcox!"

The party had come to a standstill while this was going on, and when Sweeney began his introduction of Kent—"I stand here in all humility to present to you a true son of civil engineering, a Connecticuter who has always"—the other guests began seeking the shelter of their automobiles.

When Sweeney had finished, even the Kents and the Hobcoxes had taken the opportunity to slip into the night. Mrs. Sweeney got Sweeney to bed quietly enough at last, and it has been quiet over there since. She says Sweeney is still sleeping. She says the doctor advised her to tell Sweeney when he wakes up that there was never any convention, that Sweeney just dreamed it, that everything is all right now.

Sweeney's neighbors hope it will work.

....

When the political barrier against women Presidents finally falls, some unfortunate husband will have to accustom himself to the lugubrious job of being the First Gentleman. The question that will then be posed is as old as soap opera: Can this country produce a man capable of making a woman a good wife?

SEPTEMBER

THE MONTH of September takes its name from the Latin word septem, meaning "seven," which makes it easy for Latin scholars to deduce that September is the ninth month of the year.

SEPTEMBER

····· 6 ·····

Labor Day

It is not surprising that modern children tend to look blank and dispirited when informed that they will someday have to "go to work and make a living." The problem is that they cannot visualize what work is in corporate America.

Not so long ago, when a parent said he was off to work, the child knew very well what was about to happen. His parent was going to make something or fix something. The parent could take his offspring to his place of business and let him watch while he repaired a buggy or built a table.

When a child asked, "What kind of work do you do, Daddy?" his father could answer in terms that a child could come to grips with. "I fix steam engines." "I make horse collars."

Well, a few fathers still fix engines and build things,

but most do not. Nowadays, most fathers sit in glass buildings performing tasks that are absolutely incomprehensible to children. The answers they give when asked, "What kind of work do you do, Daddy?" are likely to be utterly mystifying to a child.

"I sell space." "I do market research." "I am a data processor." "I am in public relations." "I am a systems analyst." Such explanations must seem nonsense to a child. How can he possibly envision anyone analyzing a system or researching a market?

Even grown men who do market research have trouble visualizing what a public relations man does with his day, and it is a safe bet that the average systems analyst is as baffled about what a space salesman does at the shop as the average space salesman is about the tools needed to analyze a system.

In the common everyday job, nothing is made any more. Things are now made by machines. Very little is repaired. The machines that make things make them in such a fashion that they will quickly fall apart in such a way that repairs will be prohibitively expensive. Thus the buyer is encouraged to throw the thing away and buy a new one. In effect, the machines are making junk.

The handful of people remotely associated with these machines can, of course, tell their inquisitive children "Daddy makes junk." Most of the work force, however, is too remote from junk production to sense any contribution to the industry. What do these people do?

Consider the typical twelve-story glass building in the typical American city. Nothing is being made in this building and nothing is being repaired, including the building itself. Constructed as a piece of junk, the building will be discarded when it wears out, and another piece of junk will be set in its place.

Still, the building is filled with people who think of themselves as working. At any given moment during the day perhaps one-third of them will be talking into telephones. Most of these conversations will be about paper, for paper is what occupies nearly everyone in this building.

Some jobs in the building require men to fill paper with words. There are persons who type neatly on paper and persons who read paper and jot notes in the margins. Some persons make copies of paper and other persons deliver paper. There are persons who file paper and persons who unfile paper.

Some persons mail paper. Some persons telephone other persons and ask that paper be sent to them. Others telephone to ascertain the whereabouts of paper. Some persons confer about paper. In the grandest offices, men approve of some paper and disapprove of other paper.

The elevators are filled throughout the day with young men carrying paper from floor to floor and with vital men carrying paper to be discussed with other vital men.

What is a child to make of all this? His father may be so eminent that he lunches with other men about paper. Suppose he brings his son to work to give the boy some idea of what work is all about. What does the boy see happening?

His father calls for paper. He reads paper. Perhaps he

scowls at paper. Perhaps he makes an angry red mark on paper. He telephones another man and says they had better lunch over paper.

At lunch they talk about paper. Back at the office, the father orders the paper retyped and reproduced in quintuplicate, and then sent to another man for comparison with paper that was reproduced in triplicate last year.

Imagine his poor son afterwards mulling over the mysteries of work with a friend, who asks him, "What's your father do?" What can the boy reply? "It beats me," perhaps, if he is not very observant. Or if he is, "Something that has to do with making junk, I think. Same as everybody else."

··············

INSIDE FACTS ABOUT PROGRESS (3)

There is actually far less progress than most people suspect. In the year 1894 there was absolutely no progress whatsoever anyplace on earth, in spite of what a lot of people thought at the time.

SEPTEMBER

····· **14** ·····

The children are back in school. The helpful parent is staying up nights, later and later.

Has anyone else here been dragooned recently into doing the children's algebra homework? If so, you, sir or madame, may have also made a curious discovery; to wit, that there is another country somewhere—perhaps in our very midst—whose people are no more like you and me than an orangutan is like the Rock of Gibraltar.

This discovery was made at our house the other night in the midst of problem No. 3 on page 164. Blood pressure had been rising right along with befuddlement in the vain struggle to understand Bill, the protagonist of problem No. 3.

Memory has already failed on the particulars—and no wonder—but Bill had said something more or less like this: "Two years ago I was one-third the age of my father. Six years from now I will be half as old as he is. If the ages of both my mother and my father at the time of my birth totaled forty-nine, and he was two years older than she was, how old am I?"

A number of simple computations had suggested that

Bill was three times as old as his father. "That's silly," said the boy whose task it was to solve this ridiculous problem for himself. "How could anybody be three times as old as his father?"

A devastating question, one would have conceded under normal circumstances. But not in this situation.

Here is a child—Billy—who knows the total age of his two parents at the time of his birth, who knows what the ratio of his age to his father's was two years ago and what it will be six years hence. And yet, though informed about ages in all this uninteresting, irrelevant, absurd and incredible detail, he does not know his own age at this very moment!

We are obviously operating in an odd world not our own, a place where the improbable is commonplace. Why then is it unreasonable to assume that this strange Billy may be three times as old as his father?

The fact about algebra which we begin to glimpse here is that it is far more stimulating as geography than as mathematics. What absurd tasks the people of Algebraland constantly perform.

Here, for example, is Mr. Smith in a nut shop. He sees peanuts at 65 cents a pound. He sees cashews at $1.25 a pound. Smith wants some peanuts and some cashews, just as you and I probably would if we were in that shop.

Does he say, "Give me a half-pound of peanuts and a half-pound of cashews," as any sane person would do? In Algebraland no one ever behaves that sensibly. What Smith says goes something like this:

"Mix me enough peanuts at 65 cents a pound with enough cashews at $1.25 a pound so that I will have four pounds of mixed nuts worth $3.79."

If it isn't nuts that the folks of Algebraland are trying to get mixed in just the right proportion, then it's fertilizers with nitrates. They are forever trying to puzzle out how much fertilizer with 7 percent nitrate and how much fertilizer with 20 percent nitrate must be mixed to produce four tons of fertilizer with 13 percent nitrate.

Trying to answer questions like these cannot be an easy way to spend your days, particularly if you are the kind of person who doesn't even know how old you are.

Another peculiarity of the folks of Algebraland is their approach to travel. Compare it with ours. If we want to drive from Washington, D.C., and arrive at Woods Hole, Massachusetts, by 6 P.M., we do a simple calculation to find out what time we should start: 480 miles at 60 miles an hour will require 8 hours driving time. Allow another hour for pit stops. Answer: Leave at 9 A.M.

In Algebraland, no one ever wants to know anything so useful. They want to know instead about someone else who will be driving south from Woods Hole at the same time they are driving north.

"Look," they say to you, "suppose I leave Washington at 9 A.M. averaging 60 miles an hour, and Joe leaves Woods Hole at 10:30 A.M. averaging 63 miles an hour. How many miles will I have driven when Joe's car passes mine on his way south?"

Persons with reflective minds often have difficulty with

these problems. They cannot understand why anyone should deplete his energies trying to solve them. Of what possible use can they be, they ask, anywhere outside Algebraland?

Well, children, one never knows. Suppose, one of these days when you are half as old as your mother and three years younger than Cousin Sue was six years ago, that you are driving to Woods Hole with fertilizer containing 7 percent nitrate, and Joe, who started out 90 minutes later from Woods Hole, is driving south with fertilizer containing 20 percent nitrate—

Oh, forget it.

....

PROBLEMS IN ETIQUETTE (2)

QUESTION: What is the correct behavior in an expensive restaurant for a man who discovers the end of his necktie immersed in split-pea soup?

ANSWER: The correct behavior in this familiar predicament is to summon the headwaiter, announce in an outraged basso that the restaurant has served you a bowl of soup with a necktie in it, and threaten to notify the Health Department.

SEPTEMBER

····· 18 ·····

After the summer's grim diet of reruns, television junkies return to their sets with fresh enthusiasm for the great new shows which have been cooking all summer in California studios. It is "the new season." We flick the dial and settle back into the sofa anticipating new car chases, new car crashes, new cops solving new murders, new heroines with new teeth having new adventures with new heroes with new hair on their chests and clever new children uttering clever new one-line gags. And when we are all settled in, secure against the outside world, the outside world ruins everything, and there we all are, the great American family, clustered around the television set, being annoyed at having to share yet another great moment in history.

And now we bring you a special network news report on the story that has rocked mankind, the expulsion from Eden—

"Good evening, ladies and gentlemen. As we have all just heard, Adam and Eve have been ordered to pack their things and leave Eden within twelve hours. The news has astounded all of us who have been covering the Eden story just as much as it must have astounded you in the television audience.

"The Divine announcement that the expulsion is the result of Eve's eating some sort of forbidden fruit was a bombshell to reporters who have been following events in the Garden. The announcement did not say what kind of fruit it was that Eve ate, but, as you know, we have our computers programmed to estimate the approximate nature of anything that can conceivably occur in Eden, and we should have a projection on the fruit any minute now. In the meantime, here is Herb Hicap at Adam headquarters. Come in, Herb."

"Thanks, Walter. There is an atmosphere of anticipation and doubt here at Adam headquarters. Adam has been upstairs since early in the evening and presumably heard the announcement on television. What he has been doing since, nobody here knows. The best guess is that he is packing."

"Have you been able to find out what kind of fruit Eve ate, Herb?"

"There is a rumor here, Walter, that it was an avocado, but it's based on nothing more substantial than a rumor that Eve has always had an intense liking for avocados."

"Thank you, Herb. We are going to switch to our computer center now. David?"

"Walter, our computers have had a scientifically selected sample of fresh fruit fed into them, along with a lot of data about feminine psychology, and the projection they give us is that when the story is all in it will turn out that Eve ate sixty-three Malaga grapes and an overripe banana."

"The big question, of course, is where Adam and Eve will take up residence when they leave the Garden, and for some thoughts on that we go to Bill Rinse. Bill?"

"Where they go isn't very important, Walter. The real question puzzling Eden analysts tonight is what they'll wear. Eden is a pretty permissive place, not to mention climatically balmy, and they've been able to get by until now without wearing anything at all; but observers agree that from now on they're going to have to slip into something more uncomfortable."

"Would you care to make a prediction, Bill, about what it will be?"

"In a year like this, Walter, no reporter wants to predict anything, but my guess would be that they'll put on tomato leaves."

"Thanks, Bill. We have word that Dan Quite, our Snake House correspondent, is standing by with a bulletin. Come in, Dan."

"A few minutes ago, Walter, the Galapagos turtle informed us that it was a serpent who persuaded Eve to eat the fruit. The serpent's motives are still unknown, but speculation centers on the probability that he was acting as a stalking snake for someone else who hopes to knock Adam and Eve out of the Garden. If so, the serpent will have to be considered a strong possibility for the Vice-Presidential nomination."

"I should say so, Dan. It may interest all of us to know that our computers have been busy since we last heard from them and have a new fruit estimate. What are they saying now, David?"

"Walter, additional raw fruit has been fed into the computers since their last report, and they have now refined their forecast. They now say that the forbidden fruit will prove to have been an apricot."

"What is the computer projection of what Adam and Eve will wear after Eden, David?"

"Fig Newtons, Walter."

"Thank you, David. Wally Jakes, who's covering President Reagan, is with Mr. Reagan right now in Coos Bay. Would you get out of the picture, Wally, and let Mr. Reagan tell us how tonight's returns from Eden will affect his campaign?"

"Thank you, Walter. Of course, what's happened—"

"Excuse me, Mr. President, but we have a bulletin from Herb Hicap at Adam headquarters. Herb."

"Word has just been sent downstairs to the ballroom here, Walter, that Adam shaved and had a light meal of walnuts and carrots while watching our network news special, and he has sent down a note. It reads as follows: 'Tell that stupid computer it's going to be fig leaves. Leaves. Leaves. Leaves. Not Newtons.'"

"Thank you, Herb. Now this message about something new in aspirin . . ."

The people who object to putting superhighways through red-wood forests talk about the pleasures of sitting under the red-woods and listening to the rustle of eternity. The motorist doesn't want to hear the rustle of eternity. He wants to meet it head-on at seventy miles an hour.

SEPTEMBER
····· 21 ·····

Daily journalism in America began on this date in 1784 with publication of the *Pennsylvania Packet & General Advertiser* in Philadelphia. It was the first daily newspaper in the new Republic. From its seed sprang today's mighty giants of print, with their many brilliant columnists and incisive editorialists who bring finely honed minds to bear upon the day's complex events, for the illumination of the modern reader.

Little Miss Muffet, as everyone knows, sat on a tuffet eating her curds and whey when along came a spider who sat down beside her and frightened Miss Muffet away. While everyone knows this, the significance of the event had never been analyzed until a conference of thinkers recently brought their special insights to bear upon it. Following are excerpts from the transcript of their discussion:

SOCIOLOGIST: We are clearly dealing here with a prototypical illustration of a highly tensile social structure's tendency to dis- or perhaps even de-structure itself under the pressures created when optimum minimums do not obtain among the disadvantaged. Miss Muffet is nutritionally underprivileged, as evidenced by the subliminal diet of curds and whey upon which she is forced to subsist, while the spider's cultural disadvantage is evidenced by such phenomena as legs exceeding standard norms, odd mating habits, and so forth.

In this instance, spider expectations lead the culturally disadvantaged to assert demands to share the tuffet with the nutritionally underprivileged. Due to a communications failure, Miss Muffet assumes without evidence that the spider will not be satisfied to share her tuffet, but will also insist on eating her curds and perhaps even her whey. Thus, the failure to preestablish selectively optimum norm structures diverts potentially optimal minimums from the expectation levels assumed to . . .

MILITARIST: Second-strike capability, sir! That's what was lacking. If Miss Muffet had developed a second-strike capability instead of squandering her resources on curds and whey, no spider on earth would have dared launch a first strike capable of carrying him right to the heart of her tuffet. I am confident that Miss Muffet had adequate notice from experts that she could not afford both curds and whey and, at the same time, support an early-spider-warning system. Yet curds alone were not good enough for Miss Muffet. She had to have whey, too. Tuffet security must be the first responsibility of every diner . . .

BOOK REVIEWER: Written on several levels, this searing and sensitive exploration of the arachnid heart illuminates the agony and splendor of Jewish family life with a candor that is at once breathtaking in its simplicity and soul-shattering in its implied ambiguity. Some will doubtless be shocked to see such subjects as tuffets and whey discussed without flinching, but hereafter writers too timid to call a curd a curd will no longer . . .

EDITORIAL WRITER: Why has the Government not seen fit to tell the public all it knows about the so-called curds-and-whey affair? It is not enough to suggest that this was merely a random incident involving a lonely spider and a young diner. In today's world, poised as it is on the knife edge of . . .

PSYCHIATRIST: Little Miss Muffet is, of course, neither little nor a miss. These are obviously the self she has created in her own fantasies to escape the reality that she is a gross divorcee whose superego makes it impossible for her to sustain a normal relationship with any man, symbolized by the spider, who, of course, has no existence outside her fantasies. Little Miss Muffet may, in fact, be a man with deeply repressed Oedipal impulses, who sees in the spider the father he would like to kill, and very well may some day unless he admits that what he believes to be a tuffet is, in fact, probably the dining room chandelier, and that the whey he thinks he is eating is, in fact, probably . . .

FLOWER CHILD: Like this beautiful kid is on a bad trip, dig? Like . . .

STUDENT DEMONSTRATOR: Little Miss Muffet, tuffets, curds, whey and spiders are what's wrong with education today. They're all irrelevant. Tuffets are irrelevant. Curds are irrelevant. Whey is irrelevant. Meaningful experience! How can you have relevance without meaningful experience? And how can there ever be meaningful experience without understanding? With understanding and meaningfulness and relevance, there can be love and good and deep seriousness and education today will be freed of slavery and Little Miss Muffet, and life will become meaningful and . . .

CHILD: This is about a little girl who gets scared by a spider.

(The child was sent home when the conference broke for lunch. It was agreed that he was too immature to subtract anything from the sum of human understanding.)

. . . .

ENGLISH (6)

English is a language in which an army can be "decimated," but not "duomated," "triomated," "quatromated," or, oddest of all, "pentamated."

SEPTEMBER

····· 27 ·····

With the year maturing and starting to cool a bit, we now begin to look inward again and to anticipate golden days and good harvest. In such a season we sense a little how it must be to feel old and experienced enough to look back on life with wisdom and satisfaction—in short, how it feels to be a grandparent. And how must it feel? Not so odd, surely. Hard though it is to believe when we are young, our grandparents and even great-grandparents are grandchildren too.

Some years ago when President Johnson and Premier Kosygin met in Glassboro, New Jersey, there was a great deal of official utterance suggesting that because both men had grandchildren the world of tomorrow would be better. The two agreed on nothing very useful for improving it right away, but when they talked of their grandchildren, it was said, their effusions about the future they hoped to secure for their posterity were eloquent and heartening.

The power of grandchildren to reduce powerful men to rhetorical blubber is well known to us all, but it is doubtful that it has ever been responsible for any improvement in international affairs. One reason may be that making the world a better place for one's grandchildren is usually the powerful man's justification for continuing to do precisely what he has always done.

President Johnson doubtless believed that his war policy in Asia would make the world a better place for his grandchildren. Premier Kosygin probably believed that imposing tyrannies on alien peoples would make the world a better place for his. And thus, thought of grandchildren works to preserve the status quo.

In addition, something strange happens to grandchildren. Within a few years after birth, they quit behaving like grandchildren and soon forget that they *are* grandchildren. Mr. Johnson and Premier Kosygin were typical cases, for both were grandchildren.

Both must once have lain pink, innocent-eyed and cooing in tiny cradles and brought lumps to grandfathers' throats. Looking at those two sweet infants, the grandfathers must have resolved to make the world they would live in a better place.

What went wrong? They ceased behaving like grandchildren and, after a few years, began behaving like adolescents. What man is capable of looking at an adolescent and resolving to make the world a better place to live in? When a man looks at an adolescent, he is more likely to say, "Do as I tell you or I'll press the button."

After that they began behaving like politicians, developing those cunning eyes and artificial smiles, never giving their grandfathers a straight one-word answer, coming home nights smelling of cigar smoke, bourbon and vodka.

Imagine an aging man being told that he is a grandfather, rushing to the hospital and having a nurse present him with a fully grown Lyndon Johnson or Aleksei Kosygin. Would he be likely to rush to the press and declare his intention to make the world a better place for his grandchildren?

It is a sound assumption that he would not. This explains why a statesman's love for grandchildren is such a weak reed to hang a peace on. When a man talks of making the world a better place for his grandchildren, he is thinking of those grandchildren fifty years in the future, still lying in tiny cradles sucking tiny fists.

The grandchildren for whom he dreams of that distant, better world are the innocents he sees in the cradle today. Show them to him as they will truly be when they come into possession of the better world—pouch-eyed, potbellied, compromised, short-winded, bald—and his enthusiasm is likely to wane.

In fact, this is the way we actually see most grandchildren, nearly half of whom are over thirty. The evidence that they are, on the whole, an uninspiring sight lies in the fact that when Presidents and Premiers gaze upon them, they rarely feel the impulse to say, "We must do something immediately to make the world a better place for these pouch-eyed, potbellied, compromised, short-winded, bald wretches to live in."

More commonly, when gazing upon them, Presidents and Premiers see nothing more inspiring than objects to be taxed, bodies to be fitted with guns, nuisances who make the work of government more arduous than it should be, enemies to threaten the President's or the Premier's job.

Thus, when Presidents and Premiers sit down to canvass issues on which agreements would immediately make the world a better place for all these grandchildren to live in, what happens? Do they say, "Look, there are a couple of billion grandchildren on this planet who are entitled to a better world to live in than their grandfathers had, and it is in our power to give it to them"?

They do not. They agree that they cannot agree on anything except that they do not want their own grandchildren at some comfortably remote date to have to live in a world governed by men like them.

The trouble here is that grandchildren have an infuriating habit of getting a little age on them and then turning into Lyndon Johnsons and Aleksei Kosygins, not to mention people, all of whom rarely take enough time off from making trouble for each other to fulfill the dreams their grandfathers had for them.

....

INSIDE FACTS ABOUT PROGRESS (4)
Frozen food is not progress.

OCTOBER

EVERY FALL ten zillion leaves thunk quietly to the ground around us, reminding us that time is passing and we are another year older.

OCTOBER

...... 3 ......

Incredible though it seems, the football season is scarcely one month old. It will go on and on. And on. And on. And. . . .

As winter's long night descended we huddled around the television set and watched men who were slightly out of focus play football. Television in those days was almost always slightly out of focus. Nothing really worked well at that time; cars were always slightly out of tune and the telephone, when it rang at all, invariably rang at the wrong time and, even then, only to convey unpleasant news or to urge people to purchase real estate in Florida. There was a sense of planned decadence in the air.

Huddled around our television sets watching the football, we let the year die untended out beyond the tube's glow. Snug as hibernating bears we were, though the leaves fell in the rain and rotted, and in the dusk's early dark, vandals stole our jack-o'-lanterns from the steps and smashed them against the houses. Afterwards the wood-work on the front of the houses would smell of pumpkin for days.

Inside, around our television sets, we were untouched by all that so long as there was football. The headaches, of course, were a nuisance. These resulted from staring so long at an object that was out of focus, but they were only minor inconveniences, thanks to the great variety of aspirins available in those days. If there was one thing America could produce superbly then, it was an aspirin tablet.

As autumn wore down into deep winter, the television set would begin to take on the smell of the locker room, a result no doubt of all the locker rooms that had been projected through it during the post-game interviews. This odor, compounded of liniments, perspiration-soaked socks and overheated television cameras, mingled with the odors of the viewing room—beer, cigarette smoke, spilled soup and half-eaten liverwurst sandwiches —to create what was called "end-of-year house smell."

How happy we were with the football! The house could have reeked of "end-of-year house smell" all year round for all we cared, so long as the football never stopped. Those small armored figures executing their beautiful brute's ballet brought us exultation and despair there in the warm darkness.

We grunted in empathy as tiny little monstrous "front fours" pranced about with civilized savagery. With ma-niac's intensity we mastered a language as difficult as

Sanskrit, and when we talked to each other, which was not often, such was the totality of our concentration, it was in a gibberish about "post patterns," "clotheslining," "face-masking," "blind sides," "weak sides," "strong sides," "red dogs." Deliriums of expertise—we lived in them and (like strategic thinkers, sociologists and economists) knew the sweet comfort of talking an insider's tongue.

But, oh, how dreary life seemed on those days when there was not a game to be found anywhere on the television set. For days we would watch football, breathing in contentment, warm in each other's body heat, inhaling the good locker-room aroma that came off the tube.

It did not matter that the aroma was slightly out of focus, so long as there was a game, or a pregame show, or a postgame wrap-up, or a special on the history of football, or a scoreboard rundown, or an interview with the man who had executed the winning "red dog," or a taped rerun of a game we had seen eighty or ninety hours ago, or even a newsreel clip of some football player who was resisting pressure to sell his saloon.

And then, periodically, the television would fail us. No football on Channel 9. No football on Channel 4. No football on any channel.

Someone would invariably rise stiffly in the darkness and hit the television set and ask, "What's happened to the thing?" And we would all close in around it and squeeze it and pound its tube, and someone would say, "If there's no football, it must be Tuesday."

Later, of course, there was always football, until the bubble burst, but in those early days, Tuesday, Wednesday and Thursday seemed more than the spirit could bear. A few of us would go outside to watch the year die.

We would stand there in the unfamiliar external atmosphere and sneer at the lack of excitement and someone would invariably say, "The dying of the year is even slower than baseball." And someone else would invariably reply, "It would be better if there were a front four to break its back and get it over with."

The fallen leaves would lie there rotting with incredible slowness in the falling rain, which was always slightly out of focus, and we would all take some aspirin. In the air there was an overpowering sense of planned pointlessness.

OCTOBER
⋯⋯ 12 ⋯⋯

Columbus Day

Christopher Columbus was on the Carson show one night. Or maybe it was the Griffin show, or possibly the

Douglas or the Cavett show. All these shows eventually produce very interesting guests if you watch them long enough, but oddly enough no one interesting ever appears until everybody else in the house has gone to bed.

Patrick Henry came on one night near the end of the Carson show and sparked a vivacity in Zsa Zsa Gabor, such as had not been seen since she started making transmission-repair commercials. Once, years ago, Lazarus appeared during the last three minutes of Joey Bishop's show—memory is very distinct on this point; it was definitely Joey's show—and Danny Thomas brought down the house by telling Lazarus he could do Joey a terrific favor by showing him how to rise from the dead.

One of the most interesting guests to turn up in the small hours was Aaron Burr. This must have been on Merv's show. Aaron did not say anything memorable, but when Xavier Cugat said that the Hamilton duel reminded him of a story that used to be told about Louis B. Mayer at the old M-G-M studio, Aaron leaned over and bit Xavier's chihuahua on the ear. There should have been a story about it in the entertainment pages next day, but the papers seem to have missed it, and no one else at the office or around the neighborhood seemed to have caught it.

Well, in any case, the hopes of seeing somebody really interesting, like Aaron or Lazarus, makes it hard to turn the box off until the last commercial is out, and the clock was crawling toward 1 A.M. this night when Columbus was introduced.

The whole audience stood and applauded, as did the other guests, who were Joe Namath, Debbie Reynolds, Pierre Salinger, Buddy Hackett and Keye Luke. Columbus was much shorter than you would have expected and —this was a surprise—decidedly bowlegged. He was carrying a book.

Still, with an agility surprising in one who had long since graduated from the rigging to the captain's cabin, he easily skipped through the tangle of power lines and took the seat beside his host.

"Hey!" said the host. "You've really done a fascinating thing, haven't you, Chris?"

"Admiral," Columbus growled. You could see immediately that he was going to be one of those difficult guests, the kind who do not get invited back.

Unabashed, the host quickly challenged his other guests. "I'll bet nobody here knows what the Admiral's been up to for the last forty days and forty nights," he said. "You know what? He's just discovered America."

One of the guests said, "Wow!"

Another said, "Wait until he discovers Las Vegas."

"And it really took you forty days and forty nights?" the host asked. "We have to cut away for a commercial now, but when we come back I want you to tell us what gave you the idea for discovering America in the first place, okay?"

Actually, there were seven commercials, and when the camera again disclosed Columbus he was putting on a pair of crude spectacles and thumbing through the book he had brought. He seemed to be preparing to read aloud from it.

"The Admiral is going to read a short passage from his thrilling new book, *Sail On, Sail On!*" the host explained. "Do you do much reading, Joe?" he asked Namath.

"Man, I do my best reading in the dark," Joe said. "With my fingertips."

Keye Luke said that reminded him of something Charlie Chan had once said: "He who act without thinking like man who shoot in dark." Somebody—not Columbus—observed that there was a lot of wisdom in the Orient. Pierre Salinger asked Columbus, whose hair was shoulder length, where he had his hair cut.

"I'll bet there's a story behind that haircut, isn't there, Admiral?" the host asked. "No," said Columbus. "And we want to hear it as soon as we come back after this message," said the host. "Don't go away," he cautioned the audience. "We'll be back with more."

Another seven commercials later, the camera disclosed Columbus gesticulating forcibly with the host. "That's fantastic, Admiral," the host was saying as the sound came on. "Imagine that! Sea monsters! And in this day and age! Well, folks, that's all the time we have left tonight. Join us tomorrow night when our special guests will be . . ."

As the good-night applause pattered out of the box, the camera roved from guest to guest. Debbie smiled. Pierre waved his cigar. Joe smiled. Buddy made an irresistible little grimace. Keye smiled.

Columbus, caught giving his host a glare of utter malignancy, turned to face the camera. He hesitated an instant, then gave a magnificent Italianate shrug, and smiled. It was a shrug and a smile that said, "Yes, finally, I have indeed discovered America."

....

ENGLISH (7)

Although permitted to "overcome," those who speak English may never "undercome." They may "undergo," but never "overgo."

OCTOBER
⋯⋯ 16 ⋯⋯

The first birth-control clinic in the United States was opened sixty-six years ago today by Fania Mindell, Ethel Byrne and Margaret Sanger at 46 Amboy Street in Brooklyn.

Those who sneer at the gas guzzler ignore a curious characteristic of the American family; namely, that it continues to expand long after it has been numerically stabilized. Consider the Grants. Five years ago they were a family of five: mother, father, three children. Today they are still a family of five, but their growth has continued at an astonishing rate.

Total family weight, for example, has increased from 485 to 655 pounds. In the past five years Father Grant grew by 22 pounds and Mother Grant by 18. Over the same period their children—now aged 15, 13 and 11—grew by a total of 130 pounds.

In poundage alone the Grant family added the equivalent of one 170-pound man, or two 85-pound children.

Five years ago the Grants could be squeezed into a fuel-efficient car of the sort called a "compact." No longer. They must now suffer the contempt of the fashionable small-car set by traveling in a despised "gas guzzler," a machine weighing nearly two tons.

This may seem contemptible, but no amount of birth control in the world can prevent a five-person family from expanding into a 12-miles-per-gallon family. Adding the poundage equivalent of two 85-pound children was only one factor behind the Grants' car expansion.

Another was the growth of their 13-year-old son's turtle-rearing skills. Five years ago when this son, Ollie, was only 8, he used to acquire small green water turtles and let them die for lack of proper care. Now a cunning 13, Ollie has learned how to make his turtles grow. This requires a 10-gallon water tank, a bag of charcoal and another of gravel, plus water-filtration and lighting systems.

When the Grants travel, this equipment—taking up as much seat space as a medium-sized mother-in-law—must travel with them. The Grant car, perforce, has grown by 1800 pounds. Car growth, naturally, was a factor in the family's remarkable debt growth, though not so important as the dramatic growth of the Grants' house.

Five years ago theirs was a modestly proportioned three-bedroom structure. Today it is a monstrous five-bedroom creature with a ravenous appetite for bank loans.

The growth of the Grants' house resulted from the emotional and intellectual growth of the Grant children. For example, their 15-year-old daughter, Theodosia, having grown from the quiet innocence of 10 to the age of courtship, has sprouted a cassette player under her ear and grown a large social circle.

At age 10 she had occupied one small space in the house. At 15 she needs, in the living room alone, space for three large boys, plus their guitars and saxophones, and half a dozen girls. Mr. and Mrs. Grant, both undergoing a rapid rate of irritability growth, required a two-room cushion between themselves and the tape-deck, the guitars, the saxophones and the several large children, all of which result from Theodosia's aging from 10 to 15.

And so the house grew from a lithe three-bedroomer into a bloated money gobbler of five-bedroom girth.

Grant family growth was also hastened by the passion of their younger son, Maxwell, for cats. Five years ago when Maxwell, at the age of 6, asked if he could have a cat, Mr. Grant could close the discussion by saying, "Shut up, Maxwell."

By the age of 11, however, Maxwell had grown mentally. Instead of asking for a cat, he simply brought a cat home. When Mr. Grant said the cat had to go, little Maxwell calmly explained that fathers who sent cats away created neuroses in their sons. The cat stayed.

Being a female, the one cat almost immediately grew to five.

The problems of the family explosion were illustrated this year when the Grants packed for their annual vacation. Five years ago the five of them, weighing a mere 485 pounds, left a svelte three-bedroom house and drove off in a fuel-efficient 2200-pound car.

Inside the car there was a tiny turtle slowly dying in a fishbowl that could be kept under the seat and, except for Maxwell's cries for a cat he couldn't have, the trip was relatively comfortable.

This year the Grants, swollen to 655 pounds, pulled away from an overstuffed house in their overstuffed two-ton car. Besides the Grants, it contained three growing turtles floating in ten gallons of water. It contained five cats—each terrified of car travel—who clawed Mr. Grant's neck on dangerous curves and fell into the turtle tank at awkward moments.

Mrs. Grant's suitcase had grown to two suitcases. (The second was needed to carry the family bills.) Little Maxwell's slender 6-year-old cries for a cat he couldn't have had grown into strapping Theodosia's thunderous ultimata that the Grants immediately take her back home to her guitar players.

Naturally, this alarming rate of growth will not continue infinitely. In fact, it will reverse itself. The two elder Grants look forward to the time, about ten years hence, when they will have shed the weight of the three children and all their appurtenances, be freed of the gigantic house and be able to live in a svelte one-bedroom apartment and drive about in a minute 50-mile-per-gallon car.

Fortunately, the elder Grants do not realize that ten years is a long time that will see many profound changes in the ways of society. In the nature of things, it is almost inevitable that in the year in the 1990s, when they at last can fit into their fashionably small car, all the fashionable people will be buying two-ton models thirty feet long and sneering at the world's aging Grants stuck in the small-car mentality of the ancient 1980s.

OCTOBER
..... **23** .....

Oh, in case you didn't do it last weekend when the leaves were really beautiful, this will probably be your last chance to get in the car and go see America resplendent in her autumn foliage.

We went to look at the leaves. It is what Americans do at this time of year. There were leaves everywhere. They were beautiful.

Maryland was full of leaves, and so was Pennsylvania. "The leaves are magnificent," said the lady on the front seat as we witnessed the leaves of Hagerstown, Maryland; Mercersburg, Pennsylvania; and Plainfield, New Jersey.

She had exhausted, "Aren't the leaves lovely?" and "The leaves are spectacular" between Rockville and Frederick, Maryland. That was billions of leaves back down the road. Still to come were the leaves of New York, Massachusetts, Vermont, New Hampshire and Maine.

Thinking about all those leaves lying ahead took some of the edge from the trip. You could sense that something important was oozing out of the expedition, the way you can sense a long involved joke is not going to get a laugh.

It was important to say something that would restore the vitality of the situation, and as the car negotiated Hillsdale, New Jersey, there seemed nothing more fitting to say than, "The leaves are really lovely, aren't they?"

"You've said that twenty times since we left Pennsylvania. I've been counting, and on twenty separate occasions, you have already said, 'The leaves are really lovely, aren't they?' "

"I'm sorry. We'll be in New York soon. They say the leaves up there are really a knockout. They'll probably inspire one of us to a truly moving statement."

For reply she fell asleep. New York arrived. There were glorious leaves and creeping dyspepsia. The leaves were beautiful, but pettifogging doubt cast a pall over the windshield. Were these leaves, in the final analysis, any more beautiful than the leaves in front of the house in Washington?

From the adjacent seat came the regular breathing of a person at sleep. Were not such people to be envied on a leaf tour? Ugly, unworthy emotions about leaves began to assert themselves, but surely there was no justification for hating the leaves. It was not the leaves' idea to have people drive hundreds of miles to stare at them in their scarlet and gold death throes.

The brain was becoming glazed when the highway

suddenly shouted at it. "Keep Awake!" commanded the highway.

Obediently, the mind snapped to attention. This highway had a nastier temper than a Warner Brothers Nazi. It was constantly issuing orders. "Check Gas Gauge!" it thundered. "Keep Right!" "No Turns!"

It was important to disturb the sleeper. "I know," she said, "the leaves are really beautiful."

"Now listen carefully. We are on the meanest highway I've ever met in my life. It keeps issuing nasty orders without so much as a 'please' or a 'by your leave.' "

Just at that moment the highway roared, "Fasten Seat Belts!" and followed this with a menacing, "Do Not Enter!"

"You're leaf-happy," said the lady. "All highways talk like that—"

"Watch for Slow-Moving Vehicles!" interrupted the highway.

"You're just grasping for excuses to get your mind off the beauty of the leaves," she continued.

"Do Not Cross Solid Lines!" screamed the evil-tempered highway.

It was intolerable, and we took a timid little road into Catskill, New York. The leaves pressed in effusively. They were very beautiful and exceedingly dull. A canny old Republican was burning a pile of them beside the road. He thought it uproarious that anyone would come all the way from Washington to look at his maple tree and said you would never catch him going to Washington to look at anybody else's leaves.

All the way to the Massachusetts border there was silence in the car because nobody had the courage to ask aloud, "What are we doing here?"

The philosophical approach seemed indicated. "You know, you can't say this trip has been a complete waste of time. It has helped us discover a truth. Namely, that there are some people who get something from leaves and others who can take leaves or leave leaves alone."

"We still have the leaves of Vermont, New Hampshire and Maine ahead of us," said the lady. "Ponder that and give me some philosophy that cuts to the bone."

The correct formulation took some time, but it can now be stated: If you've seen one billion leaves, you've seen them all.

············

MISERY, SECURITY AND HAPPINESS (5)

Misery is when you are in a crowded room and a strange, beautiful woman has been smiling at you and you maneuver close to her and murmur something enchanting and she says, "Uncle Harry, I do believe you don't recognize me!"

Security is taking the children swimming with your bathing suit on under your clothes so you can get out of the bath house and into the pool before they have a chance to see your diving form.

Happiness is when the television tube blows out right at the start of the "Miss America Pageant."

．．．．．．．．．．．．

Humans deplete just as inexorably as oil wells. Why is the tax law more considerate of the oil well that is going to go dry some day than of the man whose youth and energy are draining away with each advancing year? It is because the tax law is written by Congress. In the strange world of Congress, people do not depreciate with age. They appreciate. A Congressman rarely reaches the peak of his powers until he is eighty-five or ninety, and a few have not reached the final apex of Congressional power until they have been dead two or three years.

NOVEMBER

*I WANT to tell you men about a boy I coached a long
time ago. His name was Gipp. Max Gipp. As great a pair
of eyes as I ever saw focused on a television screen. I once
watched Gipp sit through an entire week of old Ronald
Reagan movies without a whimper. He never broke. Not
the Gipper. He sat there and took everything they could
throw at him. Detergent commercials. Aspirin and
stomach-alkalizer commercials. Beer. Jane Wyman and
Pat O'Brien. Floor wax, underarm deodorant, Ann
Sheridan and Robert Cummings. Gasoline, cough syrup,
cooking oil and foot-itch powder.*

*Why did Gipp do it? I'll tell you why. Because he
believed in something. He believed in old Ronald Reagan movies. The Gipper, gentlemen, was one of those men
of whom we can proudly say, "They came to view." I was
with Max Gipp the night his brain's vertical hold control
went out, and his last words to me were, "Coach, some
day when the boys are having a rough weekend at the TV
set and it looks like they can't sit upright for one more*

pigskin classic, tell 'em something for me, will you, Coach? Tell 'em to get in there and watch one for the Gipper."

NOVEMBER

...... 6 ......

This is the final weekend of the gardening season.

The annual cease-fire is proclaimed for dusk on Sunday. Nature is to withdraw all herbivorous insects, noxious weeds, predatory fungi and other instruments of warfare against man's spirit to the predetermined line south of Hatteras.

In return, man is to lay down his hose, sprayer, seeder, pruning hook and tree-wound syrup and cease to practice chemical warfare until the first daffodil shoots appear next year. Both sides will undoubtedly try to cheat a little on the truce. Nature will probably raid with an unseasonable November warm spell that revives the roses, then blitz the shrubs with a sleet storm.

A few of the hardier gardeners will try to sneak some rye grass into the lawn to brighten the mud. Most gardeners, however, will be glad simply to come out of the line, sit down by the hearth and sob.

The battle has really been no worse this year than last year or the year before that, but then it has been no easier either. The vision of glorious landscape with which the gardener entered this war as a youth has long since given way, with the coming of middle age, to the primitive survival urge.

There is the back yard where the disastrous crab-grass battle was fought. The first year had been a hopeless time of hand-to-hand attack on individual crab emplacements and emotional scenes as ten new emplacements sprang up to replace each one torn out by its murderous tentacles.

Then had come the year of chemical warfare. With a large increase in the household defense budget, new weapons were laid in and the yard was blasted with Cope, Halts, Scutl, Clout, Slam, Strangle and Smash. It was a Pyrrhic victory. At the end, the crab grass grew no more, but neither did anything else.

Another rise in the defense budget supplied seeds and fertilizer to be washed away in gullies with the first rain. Experts studied the terrain and recommended new defense outlays for lime, peat moss, topsoil, lawn rollers, a plow, hardier grass seed and, of course, more fertilizer. Expenditures were increased again for gardening literature.

This was a major blunder, for it crushed morale with the discovery that even the gardening experts did not know how to grow grass. Some said to water it at sundown and some said to water it at dawn, and some said not to water it at all unless the moon was in its fourth quarter and the wind had blown out of the northeast for three consecutive days.

That was when the decision was made to abandon the lawn and start budgeting to have it paved with brick. By that time, of course, the major battle had shifted to the roses. The small fortune invested in rose-care literature showed beyond a doubt there was a full-scale assault by thrips, spider mites, bole canker and brown spots.

Rose-spraying machinery and chemicals, naturally, had been acquired at considerable expense. Spray the roses immediately after a rain but only when the wind is blowing at less than three miles an hour, the instructions ordered. Everyone knows, of course, that this is a conjunction of phenomena that never occurs in nature. Consequently, the weapons were useless.

In any case, the roses had been written off as lost by that time, and a major new policy had been reached to plant all unpaved areas in ivy and pachysandra. Now comes the truce, when gardeners are at the end of hope and ready to settle for ivy.

Most—such is the strength of man's spirit—will probably revive and start shooting for grass and roses again by March. We all know who will win in the end, do we not?

....

In our time Father has become Dad, with all the degradation that the name change connotes. Fatherhood is an honored estate of the mature man in a civilized world, but there is no such thing as "Dadhood." There is only dadsmanship, which is a pervasive conspiracy by the national opinion makers to dishonor Fatherhood.

Everybody knows Dad. He is a real pal, but a bit of a boob. And square. He is always taking the boys fishing when they really want to go courting the neighbors' daughters, and then he is always getting the fishing hooks caught in his square old fishing pants or losing the worms down his boots.

He needs a lot of tolerating, and luckily his children are mature enough to give it to him. They usually wind up explaining that worms went out with the N.R.A. and then teach Dad the art of fly-casting, after which Dad, seeing the light, sends them off to the neighborhood beer bust with their girls.

Dad is a delayed adolescent who is always interfering with the children's activities. He is a buffoon, a meddler, a lout and a dolt, besides being a square. He is always getting a pie in the face or calling Mother to tell him how to change a fuse. The more ridiculous Mother and the kids make him look, the more he loves them. What is happening is that Dad is replacing Mother-in-law as the country's most overworked joke.

NOVEMBER

···· 15 ····

Hey! It's mid-November already, and that's frost on that pumpkin!

What is so sweet as the first cold night of winter? Outside, the temperature at ten degrees Fahrenheit; inside, a great fire crackling merrily in the fireplace. How it makes the heart leap as it springs to life at the first touch of the match and sends the flame roaring up the chimney.

It is the kindling and newspaper that do the trick. One settles into the great armchair by the hearth, anticipating a pleasant bout of self-satisfaction and blessing-counting, and the first distraction intrudes.

What is this? The great armchair by the hearth is covered with cat hairs. "Why does everything in the house have to be covered with cat hairs?"

"Everything in the house is not covered with cat hairs. Merely the great armchair by the hearth. Why don't you sit on the sofa?"

The fact is that sitting on the sofa when there is a great fire crackling in the fireplace is no way to get the most out of the first cold night of winter. Still, nobody can have everything. The sofa it is.

But something more is needed to extract the utmost pleasure from the situation. What more fitting than a tall, cold glass of mother's homemade root beer, so sharp it makes the nose sting?

"Why don't we ever have some mother's homemade root beer in the house?" The question is not spoken aloud, because the answer is inevitable: "Anybody who wants root beer can go to the store and get it." Little poisons are beginning to sap the zest from the evening.

Then, despair. The crackling fire is losing its crackle.

"Fire's going out, Dad."

"The fire is not going out. It's just that the kindling has burnt down. Now watch those logs start to glow."

And yet—and yet. Yes, the fire is going out. The kindling is gone now and there is no glow from those logs. A weak sliver of flame dies out along the bark and the logs just sit there, cold and sullen, and then there is the hiss of watery juices steaming into the ashes.

"Wood's too green to burn, Dad. That guy sold you unseasoned wood."

"How would you like to go to the store and get some root beer, boy?"

"As cold as it is tonight? You're putting me on."

"Then be quiet. I'll show you how to fan a fire back to life."

On hands and knees, crouched, nose in the fireplace, blow until the wood starts to glow. Blow too hard and the greasy ash of newspaper and kindling swirls up, flies backward, lands on face and rug.

"I don't see what everybody's laughing about!"

"Why don't you wash the ash off your face while I clean the rug?"

The first cold night of winter is turning out to be just another first cold night of winter like all the others.

"Why don't we ever have some mother's homemade root beer in the house?" This time the question is asked aloud, almost entirely out of spite.

After a face wash, back to the parlor, brain swimming

in visions of first-cold-night cosy family all-together feelings and maybe take some of those swell family snapshots like those squares in the TV commercial. No dice.

"You'll have to go outside and get the cat down out of the hemlock tree, or she'll freeze to death." Some first cold night of winter.

Scaling the hemlock tree in overcoat, getting clawed by cat, ripping hole in overcoat—that's the first cold night of winter.

"Well, you don't have to sit around looking miserable all evening just because you tore your overcoat." The cat settles into the great armchair by the hearth full of reproach. "How come you let the fire go out, stupid?" the cat is thinking, and sheds a few hairs on the chair out of pure malice.

In the gloom one becomes aware of an expensive rumble in the cellar. The furnace is burning gas at a rate that would depress the Nizam of Hyderabad.

The children hate this sense of despair that oozes off evenings like this. "Dad, why don't I go around to the store and get some root beer, huh?"

"Never mind, son. Daddy's decided to just have a little gin instead."

"Oh, surely not gin, darling. It can't be that bad."

Outside the temperature is down to eight degrees Fahrenheit and the car is creaking and groaning at the curb as its metals contract. Tomorrow morning the battery will be dead.

NOVEMBER

⋯⋯ 25 ⋯⋯

Thanksgiving Day

When Custis Curtis, public relations man for the Plymouth Colony, heard that Miles Standish and his colleagues were planning a day of Thanksgiving, he immediately dropped everything, threw a clean buttondown doublet into his dispatch case and hopped the first horse to Plymouth Rock.

"Miles," he said, "it's a sweet idea and I love it. Only a genius could have thought of it. There's just one thing: It's all wrong for this particular colony."

Standish said the colony was open to suggestions. "In the first place," Curtis suggested, "you've got to come up with a better name."

"What's wrong with Thanksgiving?"

"There's no dynamism in it, Miles. There's no thunder. This is a big country for big men capable of big dreams. When people think of Plymouth Colony you want them to think of he-men roaring through Marlboro country with tigers in their cougar tanks. What does 'Thanksgiving' suggest? Pussycats."

Standish said he thought the colony would be receptive to another name if "Thanksgiving" created a too passive image.

"We'll call it 'Thunderherd Day,' " said Curtis. "With a holiday called 'Thunderherd Day,' you'll get people from all over the country pouring in here to see the fireworks."

Standish explained that no fireworks were contemplated.

"I know, Miles," said Curtis. "I wanted to talk to you about that. You want to have a little worship, then have the Indians in for turkey and pumpkin pie. It's a great idea, and don't think I don't feel better just knowing I represent a colony that could think of it, but believe me, Miles, it's strictly a nothing bit."

Standish asked what was wrong with it.

"Turkey, Miles! Turkey! Who eats turkey? You know who eats turkey? Frenchmen. Only they call it pheasant or guinea hen. You're living in red-meat country, Miles. How are you going to put this colony on the map by sitting around eating turkey? We'll get one of the tribes out West to ship in a load of buffalo steak, and you'll be able to throw a Thunderherd Day with point to it."

Standish asked whether it would hurt the image to have the Indians in.

"Indians!" snorted Curtis. "You're still in the sixteenth century, Miles. You're going to have somebody in who will make the whole country forget Indians. Wait a minute." And he entered a convenient dressing room and reappeared a few minutes later wearing a red jacket, red knickers, red nightcap, white beard and black boots.

"What hath public relations wrought!" cried Standish.

"Santa Claus, Miles! On Thunderherd Day Santa Claus is going to arrive right here in Plymouth Colony with eight tiny reindeer."

Miles said he could not understand how Santa Claus related to the festivities of Thunderherd Day. "This colony," said Curtis, "is going to be packed with tourists who have come in from the sticks because they want to be part of Thunderherd Day; who want to feel that they're part of red-meat country; who want to be in Plymouth Colony with the tigers and cougars and the he-men. Their pockets are going to be loaded with wampum.

"What do we do? Deliver old Santa Claus to sell them beads and souvenir Pilgrim blunderbusses and those funny black hats you fellows wear. They're going to need Christmas presents anyhow, and the more you can get them to buy right here in Thunderherd country, the sooner Plymouth Colony is going to get out of the farming business and move up to dynamic living."

Standish pointed out that Thunderherd Day would occur a full month before Christmas and that it was unlikely that anyone would spend good wampum so long before the holiday.

"You're exactly right, Miles," said Curtis. "And that is why Thunderherd Day is not going to be just one single, isolated, solitary day on the calendar. It is going to be the kickoff day for Thunderherd Month."

That night Miles, John Alden and the others thought it over. "There be no doubt," said a church elder, "that this Curtis knoweth whereof he speaketh and even foreseeth the future with dreadful clarity of vision, but the question be whether we on this rocky shore wish to be held responsible by our progeny for creating Thunderherd Month."

"Speaking for myself," said John Alden, "I think the image would be very bad."

And so, four centuries elapsed before Thunderherd month was finally created.

....

INTERCEPTED LETTERS

Dear J. Edgar Hoover:

I wonder whether, by any chance, you have been tapping my telephone, and if so, whether you have a recording of a conversation I held with my plumber, Gustav Flood, last January 19.

If so, I would appreciate your sending me a tape of this recording. Flood and I have a disagreement about how much he told me at that time it would cost to have a new bathtub installed, and if I had the recording as evidence it would save me $117.82.

With deep admiration,

DECEMBER

WHAT WOULD Christmas be without waking on Christmas morn to the delightful discovery that once again it had failed to snow? Christmas is the only day of the year that has a morn. Indeed, Christmas is morn. And Christmas is eve, too. And Christmas is also all day, all five thousand hours of it. Christmas is a piece of shattered plastic and a missing bolt and a stocking hung by the chimney with greed. Swifter than coursers its eagles they fly!

DECEMBER

····· 7 ·····

Pearl Harbor Day

It was on a December Sunday—

"A day that will live in infamy, eh, Dad?"

—forty-one years ago this weekend, in fact. December 7, 1941. A day that will live in infamy. No one who was alive at the time, of course, will ever forget what he was doing when he heard the news.

"And what were you doing, Old-Timer, when you heard the news?"

I myself had just left the Capitol movie theater located at the intersection of West Baltimore and Gilmore streets when news that air and naval forces of the Empire of Japan—

"What movie did you see, Dad?"

What movie could I have seen that afternoon? Could it have been Deanna Durbin's current vehicle? I hope not. I should like to think that at that critical moment—

"Meaning, I suppose, the start of the last really swell war?"

—that at that critical moment I had just emerged from seeing Clark Gable and Lana Turner in *Honky-Tonk*. Gable! Ah, in those days I still thought it possible that some day I might yet look like Gable, though I never had the bone structure for it, of course, nor the dimples for that matter—

"And you can't even remember what movie you'd seen just before hearing the news?"

—Because, you see, we all knew instinctively then—oh, what self-confidence we had then!—that Hirohito had made a fatal miscalculation. Gable could never lose. Except now and then to Spencer Tracy to keep him humble.

"You going to tell us again about your childishly direct reaction to the news, Old Hero?"

Upon hearing the news all the family hurried home and gathered in the kitchen to hear the bulletins read by Gabriel Heatter on the superheterodyne radio. Mama went ahead, just as calmly as you please, preparing Sunday dinner—macaroni and cheese with chipped-beef gravy, as I recall; the Depression seeming to linger on and on at our house, you understand—and seeing her carry on doing her duty like that, just as if she were Mrs. Miniver, made us all feel wonderful about being Americans together under treacherous enemy attack.

"Dad, if you're about finished with this year's reminiscence, could I ask you something?"

Around our table that night we told each other that Schickelgruber had bitten off more than he could chew—

"Dad, I'll ask you, like always, who Schickelgruber was if you'll let me use the car tonight, huh?"

In those days that's what we called Hitler, you see. Schickelgruber. At the time we thought it would get Hitler's goat to be called Schickelgruber. Nowadays, I'm not so sure, but off we went to war—

"Maybe the last really fun war in the history of war, Dad. The car, Dad?"

—singing—

"Johnny Doughboy Found a Rose in Ireland," "The White Cliffs of Dover," "Johnny Got a Zero" and "Praise the Lord and Pass the Ammunition."

—those great songs that had melody. You could whistle them. What happened to all the great songs? What happened to all the great haircuts? What happened to all the great wars? I suppose World War II was the great war to end great wars. What happened to pecking and trucking? What happened to people who broke down with laughter whenever anybody said "Brooklyn"? What happened to Deanna Durbin?

"Aren't you going to tell us about knowing what you were fighting for in World War II, Dad? Don't forget what I asked you about the car."

And Gable gone! Listen, we all knew what we were fighting for in those days. We went around equipped with speeches explaining it, for use in case we got captured and hauled before Hitler.

"Give us the speech again, Old Fellow."

It won't do you any good to kill me, Schickelgruber, because there are 130 million more just like me back there in Brooklyn, and they're all willing to die for something that rats like you can't even begin to understand. And do you know what it is, Schickelgruber? The two-pants suit and Mom's apple pie, the Brooklyn Dodgers and—

"I'll put a dollar's worth of gas in the tank. Out of my own pocket, Dad."

—Imagine yourself on the Burma Road at high noon—

"Gee, thanks Dad. Don't wait up. And remember, London can take it."

No, no, no! "Remember Pearl Harbor!" How many times do I have to tell you, it's "Remember Pearl Harbor!" It was a December Sunday just forty-one years ago, a day that really hasn't survived in infamy as well as we thought it would, you understand, but still—

DECEMBER

···· 9 ····

John Milton was born on December 9, 1608. He is
perhaps the greatest unread poet the English
language has produced.

"What is so rare as a day in December?" as the poets
have for centuries now shrunk from asking. In December
with the dying of the year, what the heart knows seems
more urgent than in November, before the football season's waning. In December the heart knows the ashes of
defeat that linger on the taste buds of the mind when
man's favorite team has a record of four wins, eight
defeats, one tie and two dreary more games to go.

Yes, December knows the urgency of what the heart
knows, knows full well the futility of hoarse bravado in
the stadium's gin-dank December dusk, hears with the
heart's ear the hollow folly of, "Wait 'til next year!"

December comes on little reindeer's feet.

You meet it first on the shopping-plaza parking lot,
there where the last tree, spiky branches bleakly silhouetted against the evening smog, was bulldozed two years
ago. On little reindeer's feet December comes crunching
into mankind's unwary fenders. Later, in January, mallet-

wielding brutes will deliver an estimate of $237.50 for the deinvoluting and uncrunching of December's fenders. But now is the time for jolly old 18 percent interest charges.

December is the women, the lovely women of December, feeling the urgency of the heart, giving themselves in passion to usurers and, in their heat to taste the lusty interest charges, crunching cold mankind's fender to make January delights for body-shop estimaters.

In a checkbook, Decembers come and go almost as expensively as an original work by Michelangelo.

"December and the heart!" cried the voluptuary Barbary countess. "Everyone talks of December and what the heart knows. Who will talk to me of December and what the body knows?"

About December the body is loath to talk too freely. It is a canny old devil, knows a nasty customer when it feels one, keeps its lip buttoned. Sometimes, though, when the bodies are alone, late at night, and the coals in the sizzling hearth have burned down to a few glowing clichés, and the bubble of wassail has loosened their tongues, the bodies may speak of December. They know.

What a piece of work is December!

How in the soles of the feet, such a tombish chill. In the running of the nose, how like a curseable nuisance; how despicable in its tendency to bury summer's dearbought tan in wan gray shroud while making the eyes to water. In treachery how like a statesman with its merry call to skis yielding fractures of the shin and ankle.

Hiawatha—he of the monotonous meter—must have sung of ancient American Decembers with rime ice on the ponds and the rich spicy aroma of grandmother's mince pie in the air of the forest primeval. Only he who waxes not slumbrous to Longfellow can say for sure.

And if he has so sung, this Hiawatha, who will strum the old tom-tom to match the song of December past with threnody to December electronic? Will the threnodist sing, saying:

December is night artificially created at 4 P.M. by heaven's man-made dome of garbage;

December is a lung full of exhaust gas lurking in a pile of freshly cut Christmas trees;

December is a river so hot with wastes of the mill that made the gifts that spoke at Yuletide of what the heart knew, at retail plus 18 percent interest, that nature cannot freeze it;

December is a blackish grayness fathering a $400 heating oil bill and a lost glove, and it is a face black with slush splashed from gutters by machines thirsting to join vast traffic jams that they too might bellow with pride of still undead batteries?

When that April with its sweet showers has made every man to pay his income tax, then do men long to make a pilgrimage back unto mid-December wherein, had they been foresightful and expensively advised by tax lawyers, they might yet have built a tidy tax shelter before the fatal midnight of December 31.

Once, listening to such tedious lament, the sage Vatsyayana inquired, "Be there nought of guid then to be said of old December, laddie?"

To which the anonymous weeper did reply, "To be sure. December be-eth not yet January."

DECEMBER
⋯⋯ 16 ⋯⋯

At the Boston Tea Party, on December 16, 1773, Americans disposed of three hundred and forty-two chests of tea by dumping them in the Boston harbor. If the deed seems only mildly interesting now, it may be because tea disposal is such a small problem in America today. What we would really like to know is how those early Americans got rid of their coffee grounds.

A Milwaukee man asks what to do with his coffee grounds. Half of his friends tell him to put the grounds down the sink because they clear the drain, and the other half warn him never to put them down the sink because they clog the drain.

Why is it impossible, he wants to know, to get the right answer to such a simple question of fact? If scholars can tell how much water vapor exists on Mars and how the

Rocky Mountains were born, why can't they find out what to do with coffee grounds?

The explanation is that while new knowledge is being gained old knowledge is also being lost. Doubtless some lonely researcher once did a study to find whether coffee grounds clog or clean a drain, and published the answer. The answer would have been intensely interesting to millions of people, and it must have swept rapidly through the country by word of mouth.

In the process someone got it backward and gave the wrong information to six other people, who passed it on as gospel to several million others until half the population was convinced that coffee grounds clean the drain and the other half was equally convinced that they clog it.

At this pass the one man who knew the truth was just a tiny voice in a cyclonic controversy. He probably died in despair. The knowledge he had given the world was lost, and in its place the country had one of its most unanswerable questions.

The result of the knowledge loss is a legacy of thousands of these simple unanswerable questions. In a crude poll to determine the ten most unanswerable questions in America today, seven people were interviewed with predictable results.

Six of the seven, all in middle age, said the most pressing unanswerable question was, could Joe Louis have whipped Jack Dempsey in his prime? This was left out of the list on the ground that the answer was never known and lost. Everyone included the coffee-grounds issue in his ten-most list.

The other nine most unanswerable questions, the poll showed, were these:

1. Should grass be watered in the morning, in the evening, or at night?

2. Does it cost more to leave a light bulb burning or to turn it on again?

3. Do whiskers grow faster in hot weather?

4. Do athletes get bald because they take so many showers?

5. Does sitting in a draft cause the common cold?

6. Is gas heat cheaper than oil?

7. Is air-conditioning bad for you? Disputes on this issue often become emotional, with the anti-air-conditioning people refusing to visit air-cooled friends, and vice versa. In England, interestingly, the question is: Is central heating bad for you? No English account of life in America is complete without a reference to the New World's dangerously overheated buildings.

8. Are weight lifters muscle-bound? It is not clear why this question still survives, but it does. In any group of two or more men watching a weight lifter, one of them will invariably say, "He looks powerful, but he's all muscle-bound. A kid could take him." Every year a few spindle-shanked weaklings, convinced of the muscle-bound theory, try to take weight lifters and end up in traction. But the theory survives, a tribute to the fact that knowledge, once lost, is seldom regained.

9. Can a pitcher really make a baseball curve? Some years ago *Life* decided to answer this question for all time. In an elaborately photographed experiment, it proved beyond doubt that a pitcher either can or cannot make a baseball curve. It is hard to remember which. In any case, *Life*'s answer left the question more unanswerable than ever.

The peculiarity of the unanswerable question is that it can rarely be answered again, once its answer becomes lost. Science can go to the laboratory and produce an irrefutable answer, but the half of the population that knows better will merely point out that science also said once that the earth was flat.

What about the coffee grounds? Call a plumber. Ask what he will charge to unclog a sink drain. If he says $33 an hour, ask how to dispose of coffee grounds. Don't do it his way.

············

INSIDE FACTS ABOUT PROGRESS (5)
Forecasters predict that there is an 80 per cent chance of light-to-moderate progress in the year 1987, but only, unfortunately for us, in the Southern Hemisphere.

DECEMBER

······ 17 ······

Believe it or not, man has been flying for only seventy-nine years. Orville and Wilbur Wright got us off the ground this day in 1903. That first flight went a distance of 120 feet, which is the length of the line you wait in today to get your baggage.

"Cattle," snarled Lusby. "We're just another shipment of cattle."

We had just been inspected and stamped at the London airport and were moving in a large herd along fenced ramps. The great jet, hungry for America, whined impatiently as we all lumbered aboard, trailing cameras, raincoats, postcards, grotesque foreign coins, passports, health certificates, emetics. Babies wept in panic.

"Cattle," Lusby growled. "To the airlines we're just cattle." Lusby is an unpleasant traveling companion, as you can see.

A hostess with insincere teeth was sorting out bodies and directing them into narrow compartments. Lusby, who is 6 feet 4 inches tall and weighs 230 pounds, was prodded into his proper compartment. It was just barely large enough to accommodate him.

"You will have to move over," the hostess told him. "You are occupying three seats."

Lusby was indeed occupying three seats. Several other hostesses and a steward came, and among us we were able to fit most of Lusby into one seat by jamming his elbows tightly against his abdomen, forcing his spine into a ramrod position and using a large sledgehammer to wedge his knees tightly into the back of the seat in front of him.

The occupant of the seat in front of Lusby uttered cries of distress in Arabic as Lusby's huge knees thrust into his kidneys, but a stewardess soothed him with soda pop and the jet lumbered out to the ocean.

A stout lady garlanded with cameras had been fitted, with much perspiring and groaning by the crew, into the tiny cubicle adjacent to Lusby's and Lusby keened in pain as her movie camera ground into his ribs.

"This is outrageous," Lusby complained to a stewardess. "You charge us twice as much to fly the Atlantic as you'd charge us to fly an equivalent distance in the United States, and then you squeeze us into stalls that would give claustrophobia to a midget."

"The movie will begin in a few minutes," the hostess retorted. "It will cost you another $2.50."

The hostess brought headphones. They plugged into holes under the seats and fitted around the neck like stethoscopes. Somewhere off Greenland John Wayne put out an oil-well fire.

"Aaagghh!" Lusby's scream was drowned by the crash

of John Wayne's fist on someone's jaw. The Arabic speaker in front of Lusby had reclined his seat, pinning Lusby's imprisoned thighs in an untenable position.

"I've got to stand up," Lusby cried, and started to. In the urgency of his pain, however, he forgot to disconnect his stethoscope, which grabbed him behind the neck and yanked him backwards off balance. He descended on the stout lady, receiving a sharp camera angle on the hipbone.

When Lusby had fought free and stood panting in the aisle, a hostess pointed out that he was blotting out an oil-well fire and urged him to sit down.

"Baa, baa, baa," Lusby stated.

"Moo, moo, moo," replied a hundred voices from a hundred cramped stalls.

After the crew had again fitted Lusby into his seat with the aid of electric prods, they gave him injections of alcohol to numb the pain in his shins.

John Wayne beat the daylights out of the biggest oil-well fire in history. The curtain went up. The crew served a snack of fodder sandwiches.

"Just like cattle," Lusby moaned as sundry authoritative men hustled us down ramps and through mazes, inspecting us, stamping us, searching our clothing and welcoming us to America as though they expected us to steal it.

The trouble with Lusby is that he thinks there should have been some progress since Columbus.

ENGLISH (8)

In English-speaking lands a "souse" may live in a "house" with a "louse" and a "mouse." Nobody thinks it silly to describe this situation by saying, "A mouse and a louse live in that house with a souse." If, however, there is an entire neighborhood living in this situation, the logical sentence—"Mice and lice live in those hice with sice"—will outrage the English speaker. Perhaps even "enrage" him. He may "outdo" himself with "invective," but we can be sure he will not "indo" himself with "outvective."

DECEMBER
⋯⋯ **25** ⋯⋯

Christmas

In reply to the many children who have written asking how Santa Claus got started in the toy business, here is an excerpt from *Santa, My Boy,* the book written many years ago by his father Harvey Claus:

"Santa was the youngest of my three sons and from early boyhood he was the malcontent of the family. Long after his hot-tempered brother Henry had gone into barbering and his sad brother Samson into hardware, little

Santa would lie around the house grousing about the quality of life available to a child who wanted to fulfill his individual needs.

"His habit of lying around the house grousing—grousing gives a boy no exercise whatsoever—coupled with a natural tendency to stoutness made him a chubby lad. By the age of fourteen, he already weighed 207 pounds, though he was scarcely five feet tall, and since virtually none of it was muscle, his belly, when he laughed, shook like a bowl full of jelly.

"I reproached him one evening about his figure. 'Santa,' I said, 'you are dangerously overweight. When you start to work how do you expect to impress your superiors and win a vice-presidency with all that fat on you?'

" 'Why should I be bullied into dieting and exercise merely because of some idiotic business fad for trim, athletic executives?' Santa asked. 'I'm going to get me a job where fat is an asset.'

" 'Keep talking, lard tub,' said his hot-tempered brother, Henry the barber. 'No business in the world wants its image weighted down by a fat man.'

" 'Then I'll start my own business,' said Santa. 'I'll be independent.'

" 'You'll be just as slavish as all the rest of us, Santa,' said his sad brother, Samson Claus the hardware man. 'You'll learn to wear grim old black-and-gray suits to make you look like everybody else, and you'll march off with the herd every morning in the eight o'clock rush hour and march back with them every evening at five o'clock, and you'll look and feel just like several hundred million other people.'

" 'Not me,' said little Santa. 'I won't go into any business where a man can't be fat and can't go to work in a bright red suit.'

" 'Santa,' I said, 'you've got to make compromises in life. If you don't want to look like everybody else, everybody else will get very scared and angry and they'll laugh at you until you take the hint and quit trying to be yourself.'

" 'From the way you talk about everybody else,' Santa said, 'it seems to me they need a good laugh. In my business I'll give them something better than fear and anger to laugh about.'

" 'You give me a big pain,' said his brother Henry Claus the barber. 'When the unions wake you up to the facts of life, you'll be glad to submerge yourself in the solidarity of the masses.'

" 'In my business,' said little Santa, 'there will be no undignified mass solidarity.'

" 'Then the unions will shut you down,' said Henry Claus. 'You won't be permitted to exploit human labor.'

" 'In my business,' said little Santa, 'I won't use humans. I'll use elves. And I'll tell you something else. I won't go into any business that makes the world an uglier place to live in.'

" 'But don't you see, Santa,' said Samson Claus, 'that business has to make the world uglier. Why, just to distribute your product you would need trucks, or trains, or planes, and they make the world hideous with diesel fumes, asphalt, smoke and noise.'

" 'In that case,' said little Santa, 'I won't use any of them. I'll use eight tiny reindeer hitched to a sled.'

"I tried vainly to reason with the lad. 'Santa,' I said, 'unless you give up these childish fantasies you'll never latch onto a big job with a corporation that will retire you at fifty-five so you can go to Florida and play shuffleboard until you die.'

" 'Who wants a job that you're going to be kicked out of for getting gray-haired?' asked little Santa.

" 'So,' cried his hot-tempered brother Henry Claus the barber, 'the American dream isn't good enough for you, ingrate! I'd like to get you under my razor one of these days, you flabby little subversive!'

" 'In my business,' said little Santa, 'no man will ever have to have his face scraped with steel by men with short fuses. I will wear a beard so long that little children will want to play in it.' Then little Santa turned to me and asked, very seriously, 'Father, where would be a good place to start such a business?'

"I shrugged hopelessly, thinking he would grow out of it with time and said, jokingly, 'The North Pole.' "